YOUR RELIGION
Is Too Small

Breaking out of a small view of faith

STEVEN MOSLEY

Pacific Press® Publishing Association
Nampa, Idaho
Oshawa, Ontario, Canada

Edited by Jerry D. Thomas
Designed by Tim Larson
Cover illustration by Marcus Mashburn

Copyright © 2000 by
Pacific Press® Publishing Association
Printed in the United States of America
All Rights Reserved

ISBN 0-8163-1782-8

00 01 02 03 04 • 5 4 3 2 1

Contents

Chapter One   Big Picture/Little Picture   5

Chapter Two   Artful Goodness   15

Light Humility

Chapter Three   The Invisible Virtue   27

Chapter Four   Admiring the One Who Cherishes   38

Chapter Five   The Epic of Light Humility   44

Chapter Six   Water Splashed in a Basin   52

Chapter Seven   Desert Dwellers and Lively Saints   62

Hard Honor

Chapter Eight   The Shield We Must Defend   74

Chapter Nine   Betting All His Righteousness   83

Chapter Ten   The Epic of Hard Honor   90

Chapter Eleven   Perfume Poured Out Beforehand   100

Chapter Twelve   Splendid Robes and Special Servants   113

Open Allegiance

Chapter Thirteen   Afraid of a Place to Stand   122

Chapter Fourteen   Into the Clutches of the World   132

Chapter Fifteen   The Epic of Open Allegiance   138

Chapter Sixteen   A Withered Hand in the Synagogue   145

Chapter Seventeen   Abusive Bigots and Eloquent Martyrs   161

Chapter Eighteen   Qualities as Luminous as Art   174

Chapter One

BIG PICTURE/ LITTLE PICTURE

The man in a dark gray pin-stripe suit paced excitedly on the platform of the Centerville Church. A great discovery welled up inside him and made his voice as bright as the colors in the stained glass window above the baptistry. Pastor Johnson told the dear people of Centerville that his eyes had recently been opened to the wonder of the Great Controversy, the Eden-to-Eden perspective that Adventists have been blessed with. He gestured enthusiastically as he explained why this big picture illuminates the whole of the Bible and sheds such a glorious light on the depths of God's character.

"It's a spectacle spread out before our eyes," Pastor Johnson exclaimed. "It's the drama of the ages, the great battle between good and evil. The plot is more compelling than that of any screenplay, the climax more electrifying than that of any blockbuster on the wide screen."

Hearing this, Jack Piercey shook himself more awake in his pew and rubbed his heavy eyebrows. Something wasn't quite right here. Where was this message going? Could this visiting preacher (from California no less!) have a hidden agenda?

As Johnson continued to wax eloquent on the climax of history that would some day project across the sky from horizon to horizon like a giant cinema, Jack's suspicions were confirmed. This man was trying to get Adventists used to the idea of going to the movies. Oh, it was very subtle. But his intentions were clear. He was on the side of that new youth leader.

Just last week the kids from youth Sabbath School had gotten together Thursday night and gone to some silly movie about a pig (an unclean animal no less!) and the youth leader had accompanied them. It wasn't exactly an official church function. But he was there, lending his stamp of approval. What was the church coming to?

Jack decided to take notes the rest of the sermon. He listened carefully and began jotting down every reference Johnson made to something cinematic. After all, he wasn't a man to make wild accusations. He wanted to be able to present facts, hard numbers.

Up on the platform the guest speaker began talking about how all the conflicts in the world would be resolved in a great, final battle between Christ and Satan. "On the one hand," he preached, "are arrayed the forces of coercion and manipulation, the power of the sword lifted up in the name of religion. On the other hand stands just one thing: love—the wooing, winsome, persistent love of God. The allied armies of Satan, which appear to be an irresistible force, are going to collide dramatically against the immovable object of divine love and grace."

Trisha Dearwood found herself fidgeting in the pew. She was trying to listen to the sermon, but she couldn't get the church school principal's puffy red face out of her mind. She could still see him lecturing her about Jimmy's "dangerous pattern of inappropriate behavior." Her boy had placed a frog in his teacher's top desk drawer. The teacher wasn't at all amused when she reached in for a ruler and grabbed this slimy amphibian instead, even less amused when it leapt onto her and almost squirmed down the front of her dress.

Trisha and Jimmy had been brought before the school board—not just because of the frog incident, they were told, but because of the "dangerous pattern." The previous month he'd shouted out a curse word when fouled during a soccer game. And furthermore, he'd worn a cap to school on six separate occasions—all of which were no-cap days. They had the dates written down.

Trisha knew that Jimmy, like most kids, could be a cut-up. She would have gladly agreed to some form of discipline. But this solemn row of school officials laid out Jimmy's missteps as if they were war crimes. They seemed like prosecutors intent on getting a conviction. And something broke inside Trisha. It was just too much. Why were they always picking at the kids? Why this obsession with "dangerous patterns"? They treated every little problem as if it were some cosmic battle against evil.

Sitting there in church, Trisha had to dab at the corner of her eye. She wished it were because she'd been moved by the sermon. But it was just this frustration, this anger. Why did people have to make Christianity so, so petty? Would her son be able to fit into it when he got older? Would he even want to?

Pastor Johnson was now doing his best to describe the wonder of Christ's Second Coming. "Imagine a sound," he said, "a sound that shakes the whole earth. It's the voice of God announcing a new era. That voice is described in many ways in Scripture. It's the sound of many waters; it's the sound of thunder rumbling across the sky, it's the sound of a multitude. And at this moment it's most like a trumpet blast that pierces every heart. It pierces some hearts with awe; it pierces some with terror."

Mrs. Gilder looked over at her husband and frowned. She wasn't sure she liked this take on the Second Coming at all. Why all the noise? Church seemed to be getting noisier all the time. The nice, mellow organ had been replaced by an electronic keyboard. Drums and electric guitars made an occasional appearance. It sounded to her like a nightclub. This wasn't how you were supposed to worship. Everything was just too loud. Whatever happened to that "still, small voice"?

Mr. Gilder didn't notice his wife's look. He was lost in calculations. He was thinking about the visions in Revelation of the seven seals and seven trumpets and seven vials. He'd been arguing with the Bible instructor for months about the details of how they fit together. And now he had a clincher. The seven vials were not contained in the seventh trumpet or in the seventh seal. He could prove it. He was going to blow that so-called Bible instructor away with a few choice texts.

Pastor Johnson had now managed to get believers up in the air at the Second Coming. They were rising to meet the glorious Christ. He began talking about the wonderful immortal bodies each of us would have. "These are heavenly bodies," he said. "So much more glorious than our present ones. It's like comparing dirt clods to shining stars."

Gladys Pinnight nodded her head gravely at this announcement. Yes, indeed, she was going to have a glorious, perfectly pure body—she was making herself ready for that event day by day. But then her brow wrinkled. She remembered going to Lucky's the day before and picking up a few items before sundown. She'd grabbed a box of Wheat Bits; they seemed perfectly healthy. But now she recalled someone telling her they made those things with lard. And her family had consumed several after supper! Gladys felt defiled. And this made her think of last weekend. At a potluck she just couldn't resist spreading mayonnaise and catsup generously on her veggie hot dog. And this guilty pleasure brought to mind an incident the week before that when she'd indulged in a bowl of ice cream late at night.

Gladys slumped in her pew. Pastor Johnson was describing the wonder of our face-to-face reunion with Christ and an eternity of limitless possibilities in a perfect universe. But Gladys couldn't enjoy the prospects. Her body was just never going to be ready for the Second Coming. She tried and tried, but still couldn't keep herself pure; she couldn't keep all the bad stuff out.

Pastor Johnson was reaching the conclusion to his sermon. With eyes brimming with tears, he spread his arms out and proclaimed, "The watching universe will celebrate with us as the Great Controversy is resolved forever, as every question is answered, as every tear is wiped away, and as everything in the cosmos declares with one harmonious voice that God is love."

As he sat down, Pastor Johnson hoped that he'd been able to take this congregation on the ultimate journey to heaven with him. He prayed that their hearts and minds had been lifted toward that glorious destiny.

Unfortunately, many in Centerville just couldn't make the trip. They'd been left behind in their own small worlds.

Jack was adding up the cinematic references Johnson had made—quite a figure. Trisha managed to murmur "Amen," but the principal's puffy red face still loomed larger in her mind than the face of Christ. Mrs. Gilder cringed as the keyboard fired up for the closing song. Mr. Gilder quickly thumbed through Revelation for one final proof text with which to finish off the Bible instructor. And Gladys grimly resolved to try harder this coming week.

How We Get Small

Some years ago a British pastor, J.B. Phillips, wrote a book called *Your God is Too Small.* It became a bestseller. He pointed out that Christians often unconsciously reduce God to a manageable size. They shrink the Sovereign Lord into someone they can be comfortable with, someone they can manipulate.

I believe that Adventists are facing a slightly different problem. We have a big picture of God. We've been blessed with a wonderful drama-of-the-ages perspective. But our religion, too often, becomes quite small. The practice of our religion is what shrinks. What we do week in and week out doesn't often live up to the big picture.

The scene I've recreated of Pastor Johnson in Centerville reflects something important that's been happening in the Adventist Church. There's a striking contrast between the big picture up there in theory, and the little picture here in our lives.

For example, we have a big picture of the Sabbath and how it reflects great truths about God, about his work as Creator and Redeemer, about his care for our physical and spiritual well-being. We've also come to see it as a wonderful symbol of our rest in the finished work of Jesus Christ.

But in everyday practice, too often the Sabbath becomes rather small. We're fighting with our kids about whether roller-blading is appropriate or not. We get caught up in debates with fellow church members about how far we can go into the water before it becomes actual swimming. Can we dip our feet in? Can we wade?

We have a wonderful, glorious hope of Christ's second coming and of the dead rising to meet the Lord in the air. This is good news indeed to share with those who are grieving over the loss of loved ones. But sometimes that good news gets bogged down in the details. We end up arguing with someone over the timing. No, their dear spouse's soul has not gone to heaven; he or she is fast asleep in the grave. We tell people that their views on the state of the dead are, in fact, the essence of spiritualism. And that's one of Satan's greatest deceptions.

Details about last day events have significance. They are relevant. But those details sometimes cloud the big picture. We can't rejoice with another believer in the basic hope of heaven. We fasten on the fact that they haven't got the timing right. We can't affirm their ultimate hope in Jesus Christ. We have to analyze just what the breath of life means and argue the fine points of innate immortality. That makes us seem rather petty.

It's not that we're wrong. It's just that our religion seems very small.

We have been blessed with a wonderful health message and been given great insights into how to care for ourselves as whole human beings. But that big picture of health gets lost in the details. People tend to push specifics to extremes. They get lost in the minutia–tracking down traces of fat in oatmeal ingredients, analyzing what ice water might do to digestion, worrying about how many times to chew a forkful of food, fretting over when salt might be permitted on the table, etc., etc., etc. Small, small, small.

Too often our religion seems to shrink us. The big picture from the Bible remains an abstraction in the distance; it doesn't enlarge our lives. And sometimes the little picture isn't just something we get trapped in individually, sitting in the pew. Sometimes the little picture is preached from the pulpit. Pastors and church officials are human too; sometimes they allow personal quirks to narrow their picture of truth. Sometimes their emotional limitations distort their message. That tends to throw a pall over the whole congregation.

Human beings long for something big to belong to, something great that captures them, something they can devote their lives to. And when their religion becomes too small, they look elsewhere to satisfy that basic need.

The Dedalus Complaint

Irish author James Joyce once wrote an autobiographical novel called *Portrait of the Artist as a Young Man*.[1] The main character, Stephen Dedalus, experienced an intense Christian conversion. One day in church, he was so moved that he just poured his heart out to God. Walking home, he saw the whole world differently: the muddy streets seemed cheery; an invisible grace made his limbs feel light. The boy knew for the first time how beautiful and peaceful life can be with a soul pardoned and made holy by God.

Stephen's sense of grace persisted and led him to consider entering the ministry. But then something stopped him cold. It wasn't some doctrine he couldn't quite swallow. It wasn't some point of Scripture that he couldn't quite believe. It was the face of the clergyman giving him instruction. Suddenly it appeared as "a mirthless mask reflecting a sunken day." Stephen tried to shake off this impression, but he couldn't. He started to wonder—what would a future confined to the holy life really be like? It began to seem "grave and ordered and passionless."

At length Stephen realized that the call to the holy life simply "did not touch him to the quick." And he was amazed "at the frail hold which so many years of order and obedience had of him." The prospect of pursuing such an artificial perfection in "the pale service of the altar" seemed unbearable: "Not to fall was too hard, too hard."

So the young man left parochial school and headed for the university. There he found a calling that did touch him to the quick: the spirit expressing itself "in unfettered freedom" through art. He would become a writer and pursue beauty passionately. He vowed to become "a priest of the eternal imagination, transmuting the daily bread of experience into the radiant body of everliving life."

Who's Got the Good Life

What James Joyce describes in this book is a young man's moment of truth; the religion he wanted to devote his life to was exposed as just too small. He needed to aim his life at something bigger, something grander.

It wasn't just his carnal nature getting cold feet. He didn't just shrink from the moral demands of a Christian calling. Stephen was caught up in an intense experience of grace at the time. He felt close to God. But he couldn't get beyond the dull faces of the pious, the sterile ritual of his religion.

Stephen was compelled by the truths of the church, by the great themes of Christianity. But he just couldn't reconcile being a complete human being with the type of holiness he saw in front of him. The goodness he saw didn't compel. That was the bottom line. It wasn't something worth dedicating your life to.

Many people in our world today share Stephen's aversion to religious goodness. His experience is typical of the path countless people have taken away from religion, a path that has become a congested freeway today. And many people in our church, many people who have gone through Busy Bee and Pathfinders and academy are on that road.

When we think of confronting the challenges of our secular age, we usually focus first on the challenge of helping people believe. Our contemporaries seem to have a hard time grasping stories of Christ's miraculous birth, of His ministry in a heavenly sanctuary, of His coming to earth in clouds of glory. We struggle to make these truths real in a world that does not regularly bump into them.

We conduct Bible studies. We do evangelism. We write books. We try to build an intellectually credible defense of the faith. We try to relate spiritual truths to down-to-earth human beings. This kind of apologetic is valuable. It's certainly true that the more secular we become the less responsive we are toward that great Truth in the sky.

But there's another problem, one that involves perhaps deeper instincts: the problem of who's got the good life. For most people, goodness is what first attracts the attention; experience speaks louder than doctrine. Most individuals are moved to believe because they are drawn into a way of life that includes certain beliefs. Very few turning points are based on abstractions. Not many of us (unfortunately) go around seeking truth. But all of us are after the good life, and our perception of what the good life is generally determines what beliefs we cling to.

Stephen Dedalus, and I assume James Joyce as well, had his doubts, but he wanted to believe. The mysteries of the faith attracted him precisely because they were glorious mysteries. But something else tripped him up: that pale service of the altar, the failure of religious goodness to compel.

And that is the challenge that the Adventist Church faces today. I believe this is it's greatest challenge: a religion which has become too small for our contemporaries. They just can't fit into it. Our religious goodness calls rather feebly in our world. It awkwardly interrupts pleasures; it mumbles excuses at parties; it shuffles along out-of-step and slightly behind the times. Somehow we've acquired the idea that we must become a "peculiar people" set at odd angles to the world rather than an attractive light illuminating it.

It may come as a shock, but many of our acquaintances regard the Adventist lifestyle as a narrow—even trivial—pursuit. Compared to, say, efforts to achieve world peace and end world hunger, preoccupations with jewelry, foul language and whether women should preach in church or not don't seem very earthshaking.

There are some things about Stephen Dedalus's coming-of-age that I deeply identify with. I spent four high school years in Adventist academies, surrounded by order and duty, ambivalent about the pull of religion. The great moral issues of my world were boys' hair sneaking below the collar, girls' skirts edging above the knees, and anybody listening to Top-40 radio stations.

Still, even within those boundaries, I had no aversion to believing; God and his Word and his acts beckoned nobly to me. I did struggle with doubts, but it was a struggle I wanted to win.

Religious goodness was the tricky thing. It did not confront me as a challenge to take on, but as a fear in the back of my mind. I was afraid of what kind of person I might turn into if I became completely religious. The few who'd fallen altogether into that state projected a forbidding image: virtue wrapped around them tightly like packing wire, faces pinched into benevolence, bodies aligned on the straight and narrow like boxcars burdened with holy freight.

It wasn't just fanaticism that threatened us. It was simply a religious goodness that seemed drained of life, colorless. I'm sure our sinful natures were a big factor in all this aversion. But there was something more. We saw no signs of the good life, or the great life; nothing compelled us. Indifference and boredom were just too easy, they were too much of a fitting response to our religious environment.

Conventional religious goodness, like almost everything else in the world, is able to project only one basic image. It is positioned in people's minds with one label. As I tried to show in my previous book, "Burned Out on Being Good," conventional Adventist virtue is seen primarily as something which avoids evil. It is avoidance, the absence of. We seem to confront a world full of threats—anarchic rock lyrics blaring out everywhere, suggestive TV shows on every station, riotous parties in every neighborhood, decadent materialism all over the mall—and we have to turn away, again and again. The world is portrayed as morally toxic—tobacco smoke blown in your face. The easiest sermon to preach is one on why our society is going to hell. The quickest religious bestseller is one which red-letters a new hidden danger out there threatening the faith.

When avoidance is at the center of morality, when virtue is a matter of continually whittling life down to proper size, then it's all going to appear quite pale and stifling. It will always fail to inspire. If a people's primary focus is on remaining unspotted by the world, they will invariably narrow their way down to pettiness, preserving their peculiar slice of religious turf undefiled.

Most religious fanatics simply carry avoidance to its logical end. Evil seems all-encompassing. Their turning away from sin turns into a frantic flight. They have to build ever higher, ever stricter barriers against the encroachment of the world. Morally safe activities steadily decrease; the "true way" of holiness steadily narrows.

And so the watching world sees the pursuit of holiness derailed into pettiness—over and over. They wonder why it falls into awkward extremes so often? To many secular people, sanctity seems a bit dangerous. You just can't pursue it too zealously. They conclude that a little goodness goes a long way.

I believe there is something better, something far better we can show the world. And I believe our big picture of God gives us a wonderful starting point. But we need a bigger religion. We need to express our big picture of God in a bigger, more winsome way. We don't want our religious lives to simply shrink, to keep losing energy. Our calling is to fashion a kind of Adventism that will appeal to the best in people, a kind of lived-out faith that will touch the deepest part of their souls.

In the next chapter we'll begin to explore how we can fulfill that calling.

Chapter Two

ARTFUL
GOODNESS

In order to develop a religion that expands us, instead of shrinks us, we need first of all to change our perspective. We need to radically alter the way we think of being good. To put it simply: we have to find bigger virtues to aim at. And we have to aim at them with new energy.

One very useful way to begin re-imagining virtue is to go back to the New Testament. In the apostles' call to holiness we find something very different from the pale, chill order of conventional goodness. There is an intense vision in the epistles, an intense passion. And it's remarkably close to the passionate ambition of an artist.

Take a look at Paul, for example. Here's an up-and-coming Pharisee who throws away society's approval in favor of pressing toward a high calling, a high calling that has laid hold of him. He is definitely compelled. He urges us to make righteousness a consuming pursuit. He never wants to stand still; he always wants to grow in grace, being transformed from glory to glory. He proclaims that conventions like circumcision mean nothing and the only thing that counts is new creation. Paul resolutely follows Christ's manifesto that we must create new wineskins to express the new wine fermenting in our spirits.

The New Testament takes on goodness with all the enthusiasm

of painters championing a new art form. That's a great way to take on Adventist virtue in particular. We can best re-imagine it through the model of making art. I believe God originally intended goodness to be a kind of art form, a highest calling, something with eternal resonance.

We can learn something from what drives artists to devote their life to creative effort. We can learn something from the way art is created and the way it works on people. Great works of art and spiritual accomplishments have more in common than is apparent on the surface. To understand that, let's look at a fundamental biblical principle: the dynamic relationship of law and spirit. This dynamic makes artful goodness possible.

The Structure That Frees

Adventists have traditionally emphasized the eternal nature of God's law. We have this part down pretty well, mainly because we want people to pay attention to the Sabbath commandment. And we are used to debating about the law as a system. In the New Testament, it's sometimes used as shorthand to represent the Old Testament system of sacrifices and ceremonies. Paul also uses it to refer to a method of achieving salvation, salvation by works. Adventists are good at distinguishing the ceremonial from the eternal, what was done away at the cross and what wasn't, which system was replaced, which system is still with us.

But there's another side to the law that we need to rediscover. We need to look at it in the light of how it actually functions in a person's life, how it actually works in the process of change. God's law is really a means of developing certain skills. It's the discipline that lies behind creative achievements.

Law is first of all a black and white photograph of what God is like. It's God in outline form. Scripture doesn't present God's law as some arbitrary code plopped down on the world, but as something inevitable, ingrained in the universe.

Scripture defines the law as good, spiritual, and holy. God described his creation as "good" repeatedly in the first chapter of Genesis. The law is the moral form of that good creation. Harmony and color and emotion and rhythm are good; the fabric of creation is good. Artists who master those principles move and enlighten us. God's moral law is every bit as basic, every bit as inherent in creation.

In the New Testament, James called God's moral demands, "the law of liberty." The law points the way not toward restriction or mere avoidance but toward liberation. Looking at that perfect law and following it is like mastering the basics on the piano or the basics of draftsmanship. Knowing these principles is what enables an artist to express himself musically or visually. He is free to perform. In James's view, liberty is not a vacuum, the absence of slavery; it's the ability to perform. Freedom is the power to fulfill our destiny, and the law is the prerequisite for that freedom.

If I sit down at the keyboard I have no freedom whatsoever; I can only bang on the keys. Without a certain skill and experience with the laws of music, I'm powerless. I will never know the joy and freedom of those who can say whatever they want through music.

The law creates a space for growth, those who "walk in the law of the Lord" are considered blessed. There's room to walk in the law; it's a healthy direction. I don't know of anyone who is threatened by the laws of composition or color harmony. Artists like Bach and Mozart were not intimidated by chord structure and scale, but eager to excel through them.

The common Old Testament refrain "Your law is my delight," suggests something unthreatening we can admire, something like beautiful coloring and ingenious harmonies. The Hebrews' ideal was to "observe all the words of the law." They carried those words in tiny boxes strapped to their wrists and foreheads, symbolizing the value they placed on living in that precious space the law creates. Symbols, having a borrowed life, can of course dry up and die. Admiration can wither into legalism; basic principles can shrink into petty regulations. But the Hebrews still have something valuable to share with us: an appreciation for the creative potential of law.

The Bible gives us a rock-solid foundation for spiritual achievement: the law, the structure of goodness.

Most artists come to appreciate structure in their work. In fact, many artists sometimes sound like psalmists. They speak of their appreciation for essential truths, fundamental forms in the world. Even a romantic painter like Delacroix, reacting against a rigid classical style, valued "the hidden symmetry . . . the equilibrium at once wise and inspired, which governs the meeting or separation of lines and spaces, the echoes of color."[1]

American sculptor Horatio Greenough perceived the artist as someone "tasting sensuously the effect of a rhythm and harmony in God's world." Gino Severini, a twentieth century futurist, declared: "An art which does not obey fixed and inviolable laws is to true art what a noise is to a musical sound. To paint without being acquainted with these fixed and very severe laws is tantamount to composing a symphony without knowing harmonic relations and the rules of counterpoint."

Most artists wouldn't express themselves so dogmatically. But almost all would confess a longing to uncover eternal laws in the world they reflect on.

The law is the foundation for creative effort. It's an essential prerequisite for expanding our lives.

Not Enough

The law is good, but the law is not enough. Another element is needed. And here is where we have often fallen short as Adventists. The law, by itself, can point us toward imitation, but not art. In fact, when isolated from the Creator God, the law can become stifling. People drift toward external details and focus only on the letter of the law.

Delacroix's criticism of boring art applies to legalistic goodness: "Cold exactitude is not art . . . The so-called conscientiousness of the majority of painters is only perfection applied to the ART OF BORING." People just trying to render duty, just trying to copy the outward requirements of the law, always come up with less than the law. As Delacroix elaborated: "Continual caution in showing only what is shown in nature will always make the painter colder than the nature which he thinks he is imitating."

The law, though good in itself, constantly runs into the barrier of our carnal nature—our tragic twist away from expansive goodness toward petty selfishness. Sinfulness includes a bent toward the dull and lifeless. We don't naturally ascend; we flop around on instinct. We guard turf, take offense, strike back, put down, complain—all effortlessly. We grasp spiritual values only by taking pains.

The carnal nature recognizes only the most obvious pleasures and quickest rewards—or punishments. Listening to an enthusiastic testimony about someone's "new life in Christ," it hears only that he doesn't do this and that anymore. The part about a "personal relationship with Christ," floats through the mind untouched. The carnal nature is reductionist. Presented with some church's doctrinal portfolio, it only sees this: they don't drink or dance.

Externals can be efficiently passed down from generation to generation. The turban-wearing Sikhs have preserved their tradition of uncut hair for centuries, the Amish their horse-and-buggy lifestyle. A certain form of liturgy is repeated faithfully through the decades, father to son , father to son. Not eating pork, wearing veils, not painting fingernails—these things snap right into a culture. People without a shred of interest in spirituality have preserved these "standards" through the centuries. But when it comes to passing on love, patience or peace—that falls apart within a few years. It's incredibly fragile.

This is one of the tragedies of our fallen nature; we don't naturally retain what matters most. We're sieves, letting priceless qualities flow through and keeping back all the dirt clods. We go for the tangible trinkets every time.

Of course this doesn't mean externals are bad. It simply means that's all the carnal nature can handle. It's incapable of truly creating; it can only imitate an outward form. It is a laborer fulfilling a quota. Artful goodness is utterly beyond it.

The Missing Element

In trying to lift us above the dull and lifeless, God had to deal with this problem of our sinful nature. On a legal level, He absorbed its worst consequences by sacrificing Himself on the cross. God in Christ took on Himself the deadness of the carnal nature. And He laid down His own perfect life as a substitute for our chronic failure. The result: acquittal, justification.

On an experiential level, God unleashed his Spirit. His Spirit was given to transform those who accept Christ's sacrifice. He attacked the hopeless dullness of the carnal nature by pouring His own creative energy into us. As Scripture repeatedly tells us: it is the Spirit who gives life. We're made alive by the Spirit. Through Him, we escape the deadness of the flesh. He resuscitates mortal bodies. As Paul testifies in Romans 8: "Through Christ Jesus the law of the Spirit of life set me free from the law of sin and death."[2] People are spoken of as born of the spirit, renewed by the spirit.

19

This then is the missing element: the Spirit of the Living God. In order for artful goodness to occur, law must be combined with God's Spirit.

The creative energy of the Spirit bears abundant fruit: love, joy, peace, patience, kindness, goodness, faithfulness, gentleness, self-control. The spirit, God's Spirit in us, is presented as a potent brew, the muse's magic: "All made to drink into one spirit."[3] To the Ephesians Paul presents being filled with the Spirit as an alternative to getting drunk.[4] That strong spirit produces expression: believers speak to one another in psalms, hymns, and spiritual songs. Conversation is lifted to art. The spirit-filled make melody with their hearts to the Lord.

Having the Spirit means that God Himself is at work in us. Just as an artist is possessed with a certain idea or theme and must express it, so the spirit-filled are God-possessed and must express Him.

So how do we get the Spirit? Or, perhaps more accurately, how does the Spirit get us? Paul suggests a simple answer in his rhetorical question to the Galatians: "Did you receive the Spirit by the works of the Law, or by hearing with faith?"[5] The rest of the epistle suggests, or shouts, that they received Him when they heard the gospel and believed in it. They heard the Word; they placed faith in it; they received the Spirit.

We receive the Spirit by faith. We express faith by asking, praying. The Spirit comes to us as we look at the Word and converse with God about it. Jesus tells us explicitly to ask for the Spirit.

This is true not only of our initial reception of God's Spirit when we begin the Christian life, but also of how we grow in the Spirit thereafter. We still need to hear the Word, believe in it, and be filled with the Spirit.

The Word is the source of our inspiration. The story of God and his saving acts inspires. We need to place faith in it. How? Well, we could define faith functionally as a kind of attention, a way of looking. The artist, especially the painter, develops a very disciplined way of looking at nature, or the world. He looks carefully; he finds new ways of seeing the ordinary; he puts things together or tears them apart. The artist looks with intensity, involving his intellect and emotions. Then, when some insight develops, he tries to give it expression on canvas.

The Word is our world, the source of our art. We need to look at it carefully; with the same intense involvement that the painter looks at life. We must find new ways of seeing the familiar, involve our intellect and emotions, and then when insights develop, give them expression. This, on a practical level, is how we place faith in the Word, how we "let the word of Christ richly dwell within you."[6]

The Spirit is really not so mysterious or complicated. I believe it is supernatural. God must be there to produce inspiration when we look at the Word. But our part is quite direct and simple. We have to look at the Word and respond to it in prayer.

Light to Paint With

Law and Spirit are a dynamic process, of course, not a mechanical two-step. We receive the Spirit through the Word, but the Spirit also helps us see more deeply into the Word. The two are mutually reinforcing. Paul told the Corinthians, "The Spirit searches all things, even the deep things of God."[7] Then he explained that we have that Spirit. We're enabled to understand God in a profound way and gain insights that are completely beyond the reach of carnal thought patterns.

The Spirit isn't just raw energy, contentless inspiration. It relates to factual information about God and results in insight. "I keep asking that . . . the glorious Father," Paul writes the Ephesians, "may give you the Spirit of wisdom and revelation, so that you may know him better." He prays "that the eyes of your heart may be enlightened."[8]

The Spirit recognizes God in the Word, not just data. That's the essential difference between David leaping for joy over God's law and those who turn it into dry, external requirements. The Spirit comes into our hearts crying, "Abba! Father!" when we look with faith, when we practice a disciplined seeing and respond to God in prayer. We look at the Word and shout "Daddy!"—finding a personal revelation.

Spirit is the essential means of turning from imitative acts toward inspired expression. We are urged to live by the Spirit, walk by the Spirit, sow to the Spirit, grow in the Spirit. God's purpose is that "the righteous requirements of the law might be fully met in us, who do not live according to the sinful nature but according to the Spirit."[9] The Spirit is the resource who turns the form of the law into art.

This is how we arrive at the new covenant in which the law is written in our hearts and minds. That eternal moral form is internalized and enlivened. This is how we get to those mysterious phrases: the law of liberty, the law that gives freedom, the law is spiritual. They sound almost like a contradiction in terms. But the Spirit changes everything. He turns law into artful goodness, creative expression. The law becomes light, not a dense code book. And we can paint with light. The Spirit fleshes out the black-and-white photograph of the law into full-color expression.

One statement repeated over and over in the Bible is this: the law must be fulfilled. Things happen that the law may be fulfilled. It calls for expression—just as the principles of musical harmony and composition do. It demands fulfillment and only the Spirit can answer the call. The Spirit moves us to turn the forms into art.

Art is something compelled. That angel in the block of stone that Michelangelo saw must be uncovered. That last symphony which Beethoven heard through his deafness must be given exact shape for an orchestra. Those wheat fields in southern France which van Gogh saw vividly vibrating with color must be captured on the canvas.

You feel the same compulsion in John's first epistle. After his opening lines of testimony he declares, "These things we write, so that our joy may be made complete."[10] His experience with grace just had to find expression in the epistle he poured out.

Possessed by the Spirit, human beings become God's workmanship, created in Christ Jesus for good works. We are "living stones" built up on the living Cornerstone, Christ, who offer up spiritual sacrifices acceptable to God. Goodness is more than just putting round pegs in round holes and square pegs in square holes; it is offering up sacrifices to God—works of art that rise like incense above the world and echo God's qualities.

Spirit and law are the basic dynamic behind artful goodness. Admiring God in the Word (faith) produces creative energy, inspiration (Spirit), which uses form (law) to produce good works, (artful goodness).

What Can We Say About God?

This is the essential dynamic that can make our religion bigger, that can expand our lives. It's what helps us center our religion around qualities instead of quantities. Conventional goodness is about filling a quota. Artful goodness is about expressing something great about the great God we admire.

We have this wonderful Eden-to-Eden perspective as Adventists, this Great Controversy panoramic view of God. We have a big picture. It's our privilege to give it expression in our daily lives.

We believe that the judgment process in heaven shows us how fair and open God is. He opens His books before the whole universe. He will permit us to look them over during our millennial reign with Christ in heaven. He doesn't just decree human destinies and demand that we accept that.

So how can we express that in our lives? In our relationships at work and at home? What qualities echo the fairness and openness of God? These great themes cry out for expression.

God's concern for our well-being extends to His giving us the Sabbath as a means of spiritual rest (and as an antidote to stress). How do we show that we know a God like that? How do we show it in the way we observe the Sabbath as a special day? If people saw a special kind of peace, a special kind of centeredness, in us, that quality would bear witness to this blessing. It is the qualities of life that speak most eloquently.

Our spiritual forefathers and mothers rediscovered the second coming of Jesus Christ. They helped to make it a very present hope for believers. How do we express the fact that we know a God who is coming back for His children? Besides having the prophecies of Revelation down pat, besides having the correct scenario of end-time events, what qualities demonstrate our blessed hope? What acts of artful goodness show that we are aiming at another kingdom?

Religion expands when we have great things we want to express about a great God. That's when religion rises above the petty and the small. Artful goodness has the power to pierce human hearts with God's truth. Just one example, just one act, can make the world so much bigger.

Like a Newborn Child

Late one evening three men conversed in a small flat in Bucharest—a Lutheran pastor named Richard Wurmbrand, his landlord, and Borila, a huge soldier on leave from the front where Romania was fighting as a German ally during World War II.[11] Borila dominated the conversation, boasting of his adventures in battle and especially of how he had volunteered to help exterminate Jews. He'd killed hundreds of them with his own hands.

Wurmbrand was not a man who could remain silent about cruelty. "It is a frightening story," he told Borila quietly, "but I do not fear for the Jews—God will compensate them for what they have suffered. I ask myself with anguish what will happen to the murderers when they stand before God's judgment."

Borila quickly took offense and began growling. The landlord had to prevent an ugly scene, saying both men were guests in his house and steering the conversation to more pleasant things.

Eventually it came out that the Jew-killer was also a lover of music. While serving in the Ukraine, he'd been captivated by the songs there and now wished he could hear them again.

Wurmbrand thought to himself: *The fish has entered my net!* He told Borila: "If you'd like to hear some of them come to my flat—I'm no pianist, but I can play a few Ukranian melodies."

This soldier, this huge brute, was a prime example of the evil that conventional religion constantly tries to wall off. He was something to avoid at all costs. The last thing a man on guard against the wicked world would do was invite him into his home, exposing his family to moral pollution.

But Wurmbrand brought Borila downstairs to his flat and began playing Ukranian folk songs—softly so as not to awaken his wife and baby son. After a bit, the pastor could see the soldier was deeply moved by the melodies. He stopped playing and said, "If you look through that curtain you can see someone is asleep in the next room. It's my wife, Sabina. Her parents, her sisters and her twelve-year-old brother have been killed with the rest of the family. You told me that you had killed hundreds of Jews near Golta, and that is where they were taken. You yourself don't know who you have shot, so we can assume that you are the murderer of her family."

Borila leaped from his chair, his eyes ablaze, looking as if he could strangle the pastor. But Wurmbrand calmed him by proposing an experiment: "I shall wake my wife and tell her who you are, and what you have done. I can tell you what will happen. My wife will not speak one word of reproach. She'll embrace you as if you were her brother. She'll bring you supper, the best things she has in the house."

The pastor then came to the punch line: "If Sabina, who is a sinner like us all, can forgive and love like this, imagine how Jesus, who is perfect Love, can forgive and love you!" Wurmbrand urged Borila to return to God and seek forgiveness.

The soldier melted. Rocking back and forth, he sobbed out his confession: "I'm a murderer; I'm soaked in blood. . . ." Wurmbrand guided him to his knees and began praying. Borila simply begged for forgiveness over and over.

Then the pastor walked into the bedroom and gently awakened his wife. "There is a man here whom you must meet," he whispered. "We believe he has murdered your family, but he has repented, and now he is our brother."

Sabina came out in her dressing gown and extended her hands to the huge, tear-stained soldier. He collapsed in her arms. Both wept a great deal, and, amid the overwhelming emotions of grief, guilt and grace, kissed each other's cheeks fervently. Finally, Sabina went into the kitchen to prepare some food.

Wurmbrand thought that his guest could use a further reinforcement of grace, since he was laboring out from under such horrible crimes. So he stepped into the next room and returned with his two-year old son Mihai, fast asleep in his arms. Borila stared at the child in dismay. Minutes earlier, he'd boasted of killing Jewish children in their parents' arms. Now this sight seemed an unbearable reproach. He expected a withering rebuke. Instead the pastor leaned forward and said, "Do you see how quietly he sleeps? You are like a newborn child who can rest in the Father's arms. The blood that Jesus shed has cleansed you." Looking down at Mihai, Borila felt, for the first time in ages, a surge of pure happiness.

After rejoining his regiment in Russia, this man laid aside his weapons and volunteered to rescue the wounded under fire.

Rediscovered Passion

For Richard Wurmbrand, virtue was not something that worldliness constantly threatens to overcome. No, virtue was something that can overcome evil. I admire the skill with which this pastor wielded the weapon of goodness. He deftly brought a brute into a confrontation with the beauty of grace. His acts were such a revelation. Sabina's embrace embodied volumes of theology. The child sleeping in his father's arms painted a persuasive picture of God's grace.

This is an artist at work. This is artful goodness. Even a disillusioned Stephen Dedalus—the young man who longed to transform "the daily bread of experience into the radiant body of ever-living life"— would have found this pastor inspiring.

It's time that we as a people moved the Christian life into something greater and grander. It's time we moved beyond our defensive fight against evil. Too often sin has become the focus of attention. We're alarmed over it and warned about it. We're defining it, reacting to it, avoiding it, overcoming it, careening around it. It's about time something else took center stage. There's something great we can express with our lives. There are qualities luminous enough to turn into art. The driving force of the good life, the best life, is positive expression, not defensive reaction. Only qualities can make our religion bigger. Only qualities can show our big picture of God to the world.

Vincent van Gogh carried on his fierce struggle against madness because he had something to say; he longed to express something noble: "In a picture I want to say something comforting as music is comforting. I want to paint men and women with that something of the eternal which the halo used to symbolize." The German expressionist Max Beckmann expressed a similar longing: "I am seeking for the bridge which leads from the visible to the invisible."

We must be gripped by a similar passion. If our virtue is to rise far above that "pale and monotonous service at the altar" we must be captured by that drive to express something in our lives, to become a bridge between the seen and the unseen. There have been men and women through history who've gone beyond conventional religious goodness and demonstrated a robust, colorful virtue that awed their contemporaries. They have left us a gallery of artful goodness. In the following chapters we'll meet some of these artists of the spirit and study their works. We'll uncover the eloquence and beauty in the canvases of their lives.

In order to understand just how goodness can become positive expression, we'll concentrate on three qualities that can serve as primary colors: light humility, hard honor and open allegiance. I believe these are virtues that express something important about our big picture of God. They are worth pursuing. They are ideals worthy of our life's greatest energies. They are qualities that can expand through all kinds of expression. These essential virtues make possible many others. I believe they can open up a whole spectrum of spiritual hues.

Chapter Three

THE INVISIBLE
VIRTUE

During my senior year in academy, I drove a forklift in a furniture factory, retrieving flats of deacon benches, hope chests, and six-drawer dressers and delivering them to a man named Arthur who loaded the boxed pine into neat stacks in a railroad car. Arthur seemed physically incapable of hurrying, his movements as deliberate as the minute hand on a clock. But he wasn't at all lazy—in fact, you almost never found him at rest. Boxcar after boxcar, trailer after trailer—he filled them with a peculiar intensity.

Arthur was so different from me. I was seventeen and erratically active, racing around on my forklift, clambering over 40-foot stacks in the warehouse for a stray deacon bench, dodging staples fired by guns in the hands of the piece-work guys. I often dropped things, entire stacks of dressers tumbled down on the roof of my forklift, much to the boss's dismay. Arthur never dropped things. He just kept plodding along, arms thick and solid with labor, skin darkened by labor, clothes stained by labor. He seemed to expect nothing more in this life than sweat.

Once in a while I tried to get into Arthur, but could never really penetrate his slightly nervous exterior. He seemed to be always avoiding himself, gently turning aside personal questions as if someone had made an indecent remark. During breaks he remained in the corner, out of the way, always on the edge of conversations. I had the impression Arthur was a faithfully religious man. He never smiled at the jokes of his profane co-workers. But he seemed to be reverent toward God from a very long distance.

Invariably self-effacing, Arthur seemed the embodiment of humility to me. At the same time, I could never put a finger on a self there somewhere within his striped overalls. In my idealistic youth I wanted badly for Arthur to be somebody. But he remained deliberately overshadowed, consciously avoiding any "me" coming to the surface.

I never discovered how or why Arthur was ticking. He remains in my mind a haunting image of a kind of humility that makes human beings disappear.

Unseasonable Vanity

Human beings have always had a difficult time with humility. It seems a hard virtue to get right. In fact, we're much quicker to suspect it than admire it. There's nothing like a very humble character in fiction to give us the willies. Uriah Heep, for example. This oily character created by Charles Dickens whines his way into advantageous position by making a spectacle of his humility. Readers immediately react: Why is he being so nice? There must be something wrong.

Real-life attempts to be meek don't fare much better. Leonardo da Vinci once listed his manifold abilities to a potential patron, the duke of Milan, and then ended the letter with the phrase: "Your Excellency, to whom I commend myself with all possible humility." Evidently humility wasn't too possible in the light of all his accomplishments. The Roman consul Cato, observing that monuments were being erected in his honor declared, "I would rather people would ask, why is there not a statue to Cato, than why there is." The ego polishing up its humility.

Thomas Mann was once introduced to a successful American author who groveled before him, saying that he was nothing but a hack who could hardly call himself a writer in the presence of so great an artist. Later Mann remarked, "That man has no right to make himself so small. He is not that big."[1]

28

Today, humility seems more awkward than ever. There's no room for it in our slogans. We can't say: Let's look out for number one and be lowly about it. Seek self-fulfillment with utmost humility. Meekly go for the gusto. We instinctively distrust expressions of humility. Putting yourself down just doesn't make sense; there's got to be an ulterior motive. It must be game-playing.

Humility—the real thing—is all but extinct in the age of self-promotion. And, like some dodo bird of the soul, it only appears charming after it's lost. We gaze fondly at heroic lowliness only as a museum artifact, perhaps dressed up like a medieval saint. In the present environment we hardly can put a healthy finger on it, and sometimes—on days when the blustery, loud-mouthed present tense gets to be too much—we do ache in its absence.

The trouble is, humility isn't something you can really pursue as an isolated virtue. It's very awkward to try to be make yourself more humble. The more you cast a belittling eye on the self, the more it dominates your perspective. You get wrapped up in the folds of the garment you're trying to discard.

You end up with all kinds of self-conscious imitations. Most of us know people who have a habit of putting themselves down. When I was teaching I worked with a colleague who often filled the faculty lounge with talk about how terrible he was doing in his classes; he was just making a mess of everything. His self-evaluation was so bad that basic decency required us to tell him he was a fine teacher doing a good job. After a while it became clear that by dumping on himself he was really fishing for compliments. And so we dutifully gave him compliments—without a great deal of enthusiasm.

This is *sleight-of-hand* humility. The hand that points inwardly with such terrible accusations suddenly turns into a palm panhandling for a compliment. Everybody wants to feel good about themselves, of course. But genuine humility is a result of that, not a means to that end.

Sleight-of-hand humility is something people usually engage in subconsciously. *Jockeying for position* is a bit more premeditated. This attempt at humility requires that we become very conscious of our status.

William Congreve, as the leading dramatist of the English Restoration, owed his fame and fortune to the comedy of manners. But

Congreve entertained a very low idea of his profession, regarding his works as mere trifles that were beneath his class. He eventually gave up writing to be a retired gentleman, passing time with the boys at the Kit-Cat Club.

When Voltaire, who admired the man's plays, came for a visit, Congreve asked that he should see him "upon no other foot than that of a gentleman who led a life of plainness and simplicity." This sounded very humble of course. But Voltaire saw through these pretensions. Somehow Congreve had the idea that gentlemen didn't write comic plays. His self-deprecating remarks were only a preoccupation with status. As Voltaire recalled, "I answered that had he been so unfortunate as to be a mere gentleman, I should never have come to see him; and I was very much disgusted at so unseasonable a piece of vanity."[2]

The point is, of course, why make a big deal about how you are regarded? Even attempts to be placed in what appears to be a humble bracket betray a vain preoccupation with place. Who cares? Be happy with who you are and what you do.

Jockeying for position, in the guise of humility, leaves a bad taste in our mouths. And yet, in trying to make ourselves humble, it's hard to avoid. By aiming at a lowly position we become ever more conscious of how we are seen.

Then there is *warm-blanket* humility. This variety is not so much manufactured as inherited. It's simple laziness dressed up as a virtue. Wimpy personalities who would like others to provide for them and control their lives stake a claim to it. People saying, "Oh I could never do that; I'm just not good enough," are sometimes simply lazy. This warm-blanket meekness is a cover up for nap time, a kind of failure that asks for pity. Putting yourself down becomes an excuse for inaction. The lethargic would like to be mistaken for the meek and enjoy basking in the soft light of "humility."

Stewing in Our Own Juice

Conventional humility seems to distort people, and it leaves most of us with a bad taste in our mouths. The problem is, the absence of genuine humility leaves a big hole. The alternative—the self-centered life of the proud—has drawbacks that are even more serious. When we lower our moral expectations and settle on familiar old selfishness as a guiding star, our humanity constricts. If we follow it very far we run into a dead end. There's nothing quite as dull as a person all wrapped up in himself, nothing quite as frightening as an individual whose reference points are all internal.

When everything gets sucked up into the self, the result is a kind of implosion. Jake was such a case. I met him one day hustling for bus fare at church, greasy hair hanging limp, face an unearthly off-white, shirt and pants arguing with his body. He couldn't hide that tentative shuffle of the emotionally disturbed.

Jake won my sympathies very quickly. His eyes never rested and he could speak only in barely audible bursts—sentences rushed out as if on a quick prison furlough. His hands constantly fumbled for a natural gesture that never came.

Jake had a lot to be self-conscious about. And he obsessively queried me about what people were thinking of him—right now, that boy over there, that woman glancing. He seemed always dodging some blow to the psyche.

So I tried to help, jumping confidently into chaos. Jake always needed to go somewhere and I took him around for a while and came up with dimes for phone calls and bus fare now and then (so he could wander off from home to meet reluctant friends.) This adolescent in his late-twenties persisted in asking, knocking, seeking (like a good Christian) and I responded. But his goals were always so pitifully focused on this very minute, getting away, getting the ride, getting his way, avoiding other considerations at all costs. I couldn't get any meaning out of him.

I turned behaviorist and tried to force one healthy conversation into his jittery thoughts. We went over simple statements that people make to each other: How have you been? Did you have a good day? Jake wasn't retarded, but his feverish concentration on the thing he wanted right now consumed all normal interaction. We managed a few spurts of dialogue, but I just couldn't get him to show a flicker of interest in another human being.

Jake turned out to be a heartbreaking, maddening tragedy. He manipulated total strangers for all they were worth without the briefest introduction. He was forever running away from the horror of himself, forever caught more deeply in it.

Of course I and others recommended counseling. But he was deathly afraid of it, terrified that those smooth-talkers only wanted a reason to lock him up. We begged and assured and bribed and set up meetings and threatened, to no avail. He promised and lied (the two seemed indistinguishable) his way from one moment's ricochet to the next.

Jake was the most self-centered person I have ever known, and the most profoundly disturbed. I don't think that's a coincidence.

In Ibsen's "Peer Gynt," the mad director of an asylum declares:

"We're ourselves and nothing but ourselves
We speed full sail ahead as ourselves,
We shut ourselves up in a keg of self.
We stew in our own juice . . .
And get seasoned in a well of self.
. . . There are no thoughts or sorrows outside our own;"

Selfishness can lead us to its own nightmares. The self is not quite that divine source of light, truth, and guidance that pop religion has made it out to be. Wholeness involves getting out of ourselves to a certain extent.

So this is our dilemma. We badly need to escape the self-centered life of the proud. We don't want everything to implode into the self. But a healthy kind of humility seems as elusive as shadows at midnight. Gazing around at our present environment, there seems to be no way to get there from here. The more we try to focus on our "low" position, the more darkly self-centered we become.

How do we escape the two tragedies of Arthur and Jake?

A man named Charles de Foucauld suggests an answer. I believe he modeled it brilliantly, in fact. He's an example far removed from our Adventist heritage who just might open our eyes to new possibilities.

The Pig, The Snob, The Pioneer

In an old scratchy photograph, you can see Charles de Foucauld at the age of six, dressed in hunting costume and holding a toy gun, staring out at the world, sulky and truculent. That faded image proved to be prophetic. Through the rest of his childhood Charles established a record as a violent-tempered and domineering boy. He grew into a fat, slothful adolescent. Sent to a Jesuit boarding school in Paris, he became (from a later perspective): "Wholly an egotist, wholly vain, totally impious." He was expelled, though politely because he came from a good family.

At twenty-one, having made a clean break with religion, Charles became a sub-lieutenant with the hussars. Military duties were light, and he had lots of money with which to entertain friends in a richly furnished apartment. He showed off a succession of expensive mistresses at lavish parties.

Charles's good-time companions who admired his indulgences nicknamed him after the fort where he had trained—St. Cyr, which means "the pig." He was a pig and also a snob. When a friend suggested he install his mistress Mimi at his personal hotel suite, Charles objected indignantly: "A fox is a foul beast, but even he doesn't sully his earth, nor does a de Foucauld his family."

Years later Charles would recall, "I felt a painful void, an anguish and a sorrow . . . each evening as soon as I found myself alone in my apartment; it was this that held me dumb, depressed, during what people call entertainments." Still, the sub-lieutenant managed to keep the swirl around him going for some time.

When fighting broke out in Morocco, Charles galloped in with the hussars to establish order. While stationed there he continued to indulge his appetites, but also became interested in the Koran and its manly religion of Islam—total surrender to the will of God. It offered such a contrast, in that harsh desert land, to his own life of soft pleasures.

Back in Paris on leave, the cavalryman rediscovered his family. They were more than just French aristocrats. He realized they possessed an intelligent, cultured piety that attracted him. Charles especially noticed his cousin Marie. What a beautiful person she was, so different from himself. Marie always seemed to make the Christian life a delight and an adventure. One day he told her wistfully, "How lucky you are in your faith."

But that "luck" was making its way steadily toward him. Charles began dropping into churches to check up on the faith he'd abandoned. He was moved to repeat one brief request: "My God, if You exist, make me know You."

One evening, a popular clergyman named Abbe Huvelin came to the de Foucauld home. Charles liked his combination of spirituality and intelligence right away. While they were conversing, a lady came up and gushed, "Oh, M. l'Abbe, you always look so happy! I wish you would let us into your secret."

Huvelin, who was crippled with rheumatism, replied, "I've found that the way to happiness is, indeed, very simple."

"What is it?" the lady asked eagerly.

"It is to deprive oneself of joys, madame," the priest said with a smile. Huvelin went on to explain that religion isn't just something to give comfort. Even Christ in Gethsemane wasn't just comforted; He was fortified to endure the trial. For Charles, listening intently, these words seemed to him the perfect moral challenge, something as nobly pure as the North African desert he'd come to love.

Soon after, Charles confessed his sins and received communion. With the help of Huvelin, he clambered over the remaining intellectual obstacles to faith and then fell under the spell of an Almighty perspective: "As soon as I believed there was a God, I knew I could not do otherwise than to live only for Him. God is so great! There is such a difference between God and all that is not He."

Finally Charles had found something big enough to consume his vanity and overpower his big ego. He'd found an exit from the pettiness of the proud. Eventually Charles expressed this radical deliverance by serving as a Trappist monk in the Sahara and adopting a simple lifestyle.

In the middle of the desert near a lonely French army post, he built a rustic chapel of palm beams. "Very poor," Charles admitted, "but harmonious and pretty." Four palm trunks held up the roof; a paraffin lamp threw light on the altar. On a sheet of white calico he painted a large figure of Christ "stretching out His arms to embrace, to clasp, to call all men, and give Himself for all." Later Charles added to the chapel a few cells for guests and an infirmary.

And there he cloistered himself, marking out his island of devotion with a circle of pebbles. He rose in the dark early hours to pray and meditate, then received visitors, greeting them at the door dressed in white gandourah (the flowing robe of the desert people) on which he'd sewn a red cross and heart. Quite a few Arab tribesmen and French soldiers came to see this unusual pioneer. Many of the poor came too. He gave them barley and dates and picked up their language rather quickly.[3]

Not Duty, But Devotion

Charles had something in mind beyond meditation. His was a missionary outpost, an evangelistic strategy. He had become aware that in the vast Sahara there were only a dozen missionaries. So Charles determined to offer the divine Banquet "not to the relatives and to the rich but to the lame, the blind, and the poor." No people seemed more spiritually abandoned to him than the nomads of the Sahara. Charles set about to "love them with that all-powerful love that can make itself loved" and "pray for them with a heart warm enough to bring down upon them from God a superabundance of graces." That, he was assured, would result in their conversion.

Charles embarked on excursions out to desert settlements and encountered proud, veiled Touareg warriors, as well as hungry nomads afflicted with ulcerated eyes, malaria, typhus, and gangrenous cuts. Slowly the Trappist earned their trust. They came to delight in this wiry, holy man who spoke their language, required neither flattery nor gifts, but happily bestowed medicines, soap, flour, sugar, tea, and needles. One woman whose child Charles had saved from death, declared, "How terrible it is to think of a man so good, so charitable, going to hell because he is not a Muslim!"

Among those who came to the chapel to chat were black slaves. They displayed raw ankles, chained wrists, cheeks branded like a camel's, and backs scarred from lashes. Charles could not be silent. This penniless missionary began begging and cajoling his superiors for money so he could purchase slaves and set them free. More importantly perhaps, he wrote influential friends in France, urging them to start a campaign pressuring Parliament to have the slaves declared paid servants. "It is the greatest sore of this country," he wrote. "They are subjected to daily beatings, gross overwork, and if they attempt to escape they are shot in both legs. And when their work is done, they are expected to roam around and pick up what food they can find. There is no remedy but enfranchisement; slavery must be abolished. . . . No economic or political reasons countenance such immorality, such hideous injustice."

It's remarkable how far out of his fat, indulgent, vain little self this man had traveled. He'd grown up amid aristocratic ease but endured the harsh desert with an easy cheerfulness. Charles explained that, in prayer, he saw that his Lord was infinitely happy and lacked nothing—"Then I, too, am happy, and I lack nothing; Your happiness suffices me." He came to possess an unshakable sense of self-in-Christ. And this enabled him to greatly expand his identity. Charles could live among the North African Arabs as one of them.

In time he would translate over 6,000 verses of Touareg poetry. Working patiently to render meter and idiom of these love songs in flawless, clear French, he created one of the world's great anthologies of primitive verse. In the end he gave the Touareg language a grammar, dictionary, and literature, both prose and verse.

Charles's radical humility didn't make him passive. It didn't erase his will. He still had a fire in his belly. But that fire burned for a reason. Charles was driven to express something eternal in terrain of sand. He longed, above all else, to imitate "the hidden life of the poor and humble Workman of Nazareth." His efforts didn't come from an overbearing sense of duty. They came from passionate devotion. "I love our Lord," Charles once wrote trying to explain why he became a Trappist, "and since I love Him, I cannot bear to live a different life from His, an easy and honoured life when his was the hardest and most despised that has ever been." Another clergyman noticed him on several occasions spending an entire night kneeling in the church "conversing with his beloved Jesus . . . his face shining with a gentle joy."

This intimacy with His Lord gave Charles a profound security in His calling. Through his simple lifestyle he was making his own statement as an artist of the spirit. He never insisted that others copy him. When he sent a young Touareg to France for a visit, he carefully arranged that everything be pleasant and comfortable for him there. While traveling with a certain Brother Michael, Charles would cover him with his own cloak during the night, explaining to others that he was hardened to the desert cold. He provided barley cake for the man each morning, though he never had breakfast.

Charles submitted to a demanding religious discipline, but his centering all on God made it seem effortless. "He holds up equally my soul and my body;" he assured friends. "I have nothing to carry, He carries it all."

On rare occasions, when Charles found someone who could understand something of his feelings, he tried to share "the immense happiness which one enjoys at the thought that God is God and that He whom we love with our whole being is infinitely and eternally blessed." This is the theme you find over and over in his letters. Charles was intensely happy that God is God. He feels "drowned in God." Here was someone rejoicing not just in God's blessings but in God Himself. He wasn't just devoted to a sublime feeling in the soul, but to a separate greatness.

To appreciate Charles de Foucauld, you have to see him as an artist. He was expressing, through his tightly focused life in the Sahara, a theme that consumed him: the sacrificial life of Christ. To him, one of his most significant accomplishments there was simply worshipping Christ crucified. That act was meaningful enough, full enough, to occupy a lifetime.

Charles thought it a privilege to do this in the most desolate place, in the place where Christ had not been lifted up before. His adoration is etched against the mile-high massifs of the Ahaggar, the rolling sands, the dry rounded stones of ancient river beds. His worship was a fiery gold sunset played against beige and gray rock.

A member of the White Fathers once traveled with Charles from France to Ghardaia. He would recall he had never met anyone with such a supernatural radiance. "It was as though, inside the frail priest, someone was always singing for joy, so that, if you were quiet enough, recollected enough when you were with Charles, you too, could hear Him."

After Charles' death at the hands of rogue tribesmen, his life could be summed up in the few possessions discovered at his chapel: a breviary, cross, chalice, linen, and candlesticks. That is all. An eloquent still life, each object essential in the composition, laid out with passionate conviction.

Chapter Four

ADMIRING THE ONE WHO CHERISHES

There are times in my life when I've had a peek at what drove Charles de Foucauld in his worshipful desert quest. It usually happens during devotions when I really get into the spirit of praise, praising God directly. I'm moved by a sense of how marvelous and many-faceted God's character must be. And suddenly I really get it: "Yes! Just to bow before him right now, that's meaningful enough for a lifetime. To have done this equals all that a human being can accomplish."

I must admit the feeling doesn't last very long. There is much in me and around me to distract devotion. I drive on LA freeways and want to shout back at the guy gesturing obscenely who wants to go 66 to my 64 mph. I have a "position" to maintain at a big media center. Entertainment of every sort bulges out from my TV, ready at my beck and call. I am a long way from Charles's chapel in the desert.

But the one thing I cannot do after knowing Charles is to shrug off pride and self-centeredness with an "I'm only human" excuse. That's not good enough anymore. In the canvas of Charles de Foucauld's life I find a compelling picture of healthy humility. It strikes me as a direct expression of his awareness of a great God. Charles the piggish egotist met the Almighty head-on and was re-created as an unassuming giver of life in the desert.

This man helps us put a finger on that elusive, invisible virtue. He suggests that the proud are constantly on the look out for those they consider lesser than themselves, always ready to peg an inferior with a knowing smirk or cutting remark. That is the food with which their identity is nourished.

The humble, however, nourish their identity on someone greater: an esteemed friend, a hero—God. The key word here is admiration. The humble have the capacity to respect and admire loftier qualities. They enjoy other peoples' successes rather than feel threatened by them. The humble are looking up; they seek a relationship with someone greater. Healthy humility is the natural result of seeking God.

That is one reason an unbelieving age finds humility so odd. Even if secular individuals admire it in theory, it's hard to find a place for it in real life. Humility simply can't be had as an isolated commodity.

In 1937, Lin Yutang published a bestseller called *The Importance of Living* which contained a section entitled "Why I Am a Pagan" describing his objections to the "presumptuous arrogance" of Christian theology. He became a symbol of the sophisticated, cosmopolitan Asian scholar, writing books on Chinese and Indian culture and philosophy. But then he ran into a very basic human problem:

> "Below the surface of my life a disquiet, born of both reflection and experience, began to set in. I saw that the fruit of the humanistic age of enlightenment was an age of materialism. Man's increasing belief in himself as God did not seem to be making him more godlike. He was becoming more clever. But he had less and less of the sober, uplifting humility of one who has stood in the presence of God. Much of contemporary history seemed to me to indicate how dangerously near the savage state that man, lacking that humility, may be even while he is most advanced materially and technologically."[1]

Yutang's disaffection led him to a study of the Gospels. He was struck by the "awe-inspiring simplicity and beauty of the teachings of Jesus." He learned to admire Him and discovered at last that "uplifting humility" he believed so necessary to healthy human life.

Humility is a side effect of devotion. It only exists as a ricochet, as something that comes from admiring the Almighty.

Admiring Him More

We can't make ourselves humble. That's an important point to remember as we seek to grow in the Christian life. It will help us relate to the specifics of "being humble" in a healthier way.

Larry was a young, conscientious Adventist whose employer told him how much he valued his work, and that he was going to get a raise. When Larry received his first newly adjusted pay check, he felt a bit of a rush. It was nice to be appreciated so concretely. He was leaning back in his chair at the office, feeling very expansive, when suddenly he thought, "Wait a minute, maybe I shouldn't feel good just because of this. I should be content simply being a servant, expecting no pat on the back."

Larry, as a good Christian, was trying to resist something called self-exaltation. He didn't want to enjoy the boss's praise too much. In fact he'd made it a habit to deflect compliments and yank the self out of the spotlight before it got warmed up. So Larry spent the rest of the day trying to ignore his promotion, trying to protect that slippery virtue, humility, which can slip away when you least expect it.

Many believers do things like this in order to avoid pride. But this is the wrong starting point for humility. Humility has to do with our capacity to relate to Someone greater than us, and find our identity in Him. When we run away from every compliment, we're saying, in effect, "If I admire something about myself I won't be able to reverence God as much." Well, it's true that big egos can belittle God, and that flattering attentions can turn our heads away from a sense of His majesty. But the answer is not to avoid compliments like the plague or to think less of your abilities. It's simply to think more of God's. Admire God—that's the essential starting point. We don't have to put ourselves down in order to make God great. He's not threatened by our successes. His majesty stretches far above our noblest achievements.

So, when we're complimented we can thank people sincerely. We can enjoy it and appreciate it. We can celebrate our talents and abilities as gifts from God. Every spotlight thrown on us is a chance to beam up praise to God.

It's when people stop thanking God that egos get out of hand.

That's the danger. When praise stops here at my feet and the natural flow is plugged up—that's when humility gets shoved out.

Humility isn't something we do to ourselves; it's something we absorb as a result of being thankful to God. The best way to experience healthy humility is to admire God.

And here's where our Big Picture of God can be a great help. It's important because the kind of God we admire determines the kind of humility we experience. Healthy humility comes from admiring the sovereign, personal God of the Bible.

This is not the same as admiring, say, an ideology or being committed to a certain doctrinal position. We may regard a certain ideology as greater than ourselves; we may even give it our ultimate allegiance. But that doesn't produce healthy humility. Ideologies don't call us into a love relationship. It's easy for the self to absorb any abstract doctrine as My Opinion. It's easy for us to manipulate truth into something that just proves I Am Right.

Loving, Separate, Holy

But God is not so easily manipulated, at least not the God who appears to us in the Bible's Big Picture. Fortunately our Adventist heritage highlights plenty of things about God to admire. We bow before a God who loves us from eternity past when he began laying out the plan of salvation. He began his creation in love and he will bring all of creation to a climax in a harmonious declaration of love after the Great Controversy is resolved. Our Creator is the ultimate "significant other" who can give us a secure identity. He is the infinitely great individual whose love for us is infinitely intense. That's security.

This profound security is what produces the quality we'll identify as "light humility." It is very different from the dark humility of those trying to put themselves down in all kinds of self-conscious ways. Light humility is buoyant; it's unburdened. It doesn't have to try to do anything to the self; it's part of a response toward God. It's light because it's bathed in the light of God's positive regard.

Light humility expresses a God who loves us; it also expresses a God who is separate from us. That's another essential part of the Big Picture. Adventists cherish a sovereign Lord who speaks truth to the world and to the human heart. He makes revelations. His thoughts are above ours as the heavens stand high above the earth. He is not simply some eternal essence inherent in our souls. Saying that we're all God and God is all of us may sound encouraging at first, but it falls apart in the end. If God is all things, in everything equally, then we've just labeled the world differently; we've just put a higher sticker price on the same old sedan. Proclaiming that God is everything is ultimately not much different from saying God is nothing.

Our big picture of God has solid roots in Creation, in our being created in the image of God. The biblical distinction between Creator and creature is important here. God is intimately related to us, but He is not us. He is a separate individual seeking genuine relationships with other separate individuals. Light humility doesn't result from the self claiming squatter's rights on divinity; it arises from the self relating to Someone separate, Someone greater.

That separate Sovereign is also a holy Lord. That's another of His essential attributes that we can admire to great effect. Our big picture of God involves a big picture of the plan of salvation. God had to save sinful human beings in a certain way in order to maintain His integrity. He had to live as a man among human beings, taking on our frailty, and fulfilling the just requirements of the law in our place. He had to lay down His life in order to be just and the justifier of sinful individuals who place their faith in him. He had to answer Satan's accusations in a way that would demonstrate His fairness. God made the ultimate sacrifice in order to vindicate His character.

Yes, God's holiness should stand tall for us. God's passion for justice must be included with His compassion for imperfect individuals. The accepting God who gives people self-worth is not a moral pushover. The Bible presents Him as a consuming fire of righteousness, upright in all His ways, faithful to generation after generation.

An idealistic high school student named Ben became very depressed during his senior year. He'd been thinking about life a lot, and he just couldn't get over all the cruelty and suffering in the world. Why continue your education? Why even pursue a career?

Ben began contemplating suicide. In school he'd been exposed to ideas from pop-psychology. Acceptance was a big theme. But it was value-free acceptance—no strings attached. And Ben couldn't bring himself to accept things as they were. It was a lie to accept evil. Things were definitely not OK.

But one day, in the middle of his gloomy thoughts about ending it all, a new idea hit him hard: If there was just one man who lived a good life, a completely good life, it would be worth it all. Ben had seen plenty of evidence that even the best among us can be corrupted. But what if there was an exception? Yes, that would make a difference.

Ben carried that thought around for a while as his last argument against suicide. Then he spent a holiday at his aunt's house. This Christian woman's kindly behavior reminded him of things he'd learned as a kid in Sunday School. All those stories about Jesus came back to him. Suddenly he realized he had an answer, precisely. Jesus was the completely good man who made life worthwhile.

Ben didn't kill himself. He went on to college, the same Illinois University I attended. And there I had the pleasure of knowing him as one of the more dynamic believers on campus. He had found a rewarding relationship with this one Good Man.

It is a holy God who extends us His gracious regard. That makes an enormous difference. He isn't just some benign blob in the sky who hands out nice greeting cards to the needy masses. This loving, separate God makes moral demands. He has high expectations.

Unfortunately, a lot of people have reduced God to the fast-food essentials: He loves everybody so slide in and out whenever convenient on greasy value-free acceptance; I'll take mine without that high-fiber part about holiness, please.

But the humble sense their responsibility before a God of law. They don't just look up at a frozen smile; they bow before a righteous Lord. They sincerely admire the holy God who has chosen them.

Light humility, healthy security, has to have this combination: righteous expectations and loving acceptance. The God of the Big Picture expresses both consistently and intensely. He has created each one of us for the good life. We aren't just victims on this planet. We haven't been abandoned to some ghetto for the morally handicapped, told that it's OK, we can't make it, we're only human. No, God believes in us and has high hopes for us. But He always catches us when we fall. He accepts our frailty and forgives our moral stumblings. He is able to love us when we're at our worst—and still hope for the best.

God's ardent expressions of justice and mercy produce a profound sense of security in those who bow before Him. They experience light humility. And this humility, in turn, opens them up to more mercy and justice.

Chapter Five

THE EPIC OF LIGHT HUMILITY

The Bible gives us a separate, loving, holy God to admire. It also fleshes out the humility of those who admire. One of the great themes of Scripture is humility in mortal combat with pride. It is a panoramic epic flowing through generations and peoples and empires. This is another Eden-to-Eden theme, another Big Picture that we can meditate on like the artist meditating on a part of nature. We express the real thing best when we have come to know this original revelation.

Two big events in the book of Genesis, Creation and the Flood, reveal in different ways the God who is sovereign over the world. But human pride also made an early stand in history. It constructed its first presumptuous monument: the Tower of Babel. This ziggurat challenged God's promise of protection as embodied in the rainbow. Rather than look up to God, those industrious folks on the plain of Shinar insisted on competing with Him. *If this god is ruler in the heavens, we just have to build a taller ziggurat to deal with him.*

The story continues with roughly cut patriarchs running up against this oversized God, a God who had to distinguish Himself from local deities battling over turf. Abraham stared up at numberless stars stretching out the black heavens and believed a Lord big enough to promise the impossible. Jacob ran away from home and his own sin and found a ladder stretching up, far up into heaven. Later he wrestled with his Lord and was defeated, but gained a special blessing. These are elemental encounters, earthly nomads learning to bow.

It is significant that the book of Job—that long agonized intellectual wrestling match with the problem of evil—climaxes with the main character humbling himself before a sovereign Creator, as if that were the answer. At the end of the book we are not rewarded with a neat formula which unties all the moral and theological knots Job and friends have produced for almost forty chapters. None of the debaters wins. There is only the vivid picture of an infinitely wise God to admire. The only thing human to triumph at the end is humility.

Moses vs. Pharaoh

Human beings humbled before the God of Heaven produced their first great protagonist in Moses. He was perfect for the part: raised as royalty, but without any desire to be king; fiery for justice, but tempered by years of shepherding. Later generations would look back on his accomplishments and call him the meekest man on earth.

Moses came up against Pharaoh, also perfect for his part. It is an epic conflict: man speaking for a God bigger than Himself vs. man speaking for an enormous ego. Moses presented Jehovah's signs; Pharaoh ushered in his magicians. Moses warned of Jehovah's judgments; Pharaoh replied that he'd never heard of Him. The more this ruler's sovereignty was challenged, the more obstinate he became.

Pharaoh was plagued by frogs, gnats, locusts. His cattle died; hail destroyed Egypt's crops. But the man hung tough, unbowed. Here the self-centered man was exposed as pathological. He would rather destroy everything than submit to someone bigger than himself. He fears he will lose himself if he bows.

After the Exodus, during the wilderness wanderings, Moses rose to extraordinary heights of humility, bearing patiently with the chronic grumbling and moral stumbling of the children of Israel. His career created the first great alternative to the oriental despots who dominated the ancient world: the leader as servant of the people. There in the wastelands of Edom, Shinar and Meribah, Moses fetched water and bread and quail for the multitudes.

He managed to sidestep the traps that usually swallow up those in power. Moses took advice. When father-in-law Jethro dropped into camp for a visit and saw how overwhelmed Moses was trying to settle petty legal disputes, he suggested that honest men be chosen as judges for the people. Moses listened and began delegating responsibility.

Moses refused to create enemies. When someone came running up with news that two unauthorized laymen were prophesying, right-hand-man Joshua urged his leader to have them restrained. Moses replied, "Are you jealous for my sake? I wish that all the Lord's people were prophets." When Miriam and Aaron began criticizing Moses, jealous of his authority, Moses didn't react defensively. He allowed the Lord to settle the matter. After ambitious Miriam was struck with leprosy, Moses pled with God to heal her.

Jehovah Himself threw a spotlight on Moses' selflessness by making an offer no ruler in his right mind could refuse. When most of the Israelites had turned their backs on their leader and their God, God proposed: "Let me destroy these people. Then I will make your descendants into a great nation." Moses' ego did not rise to the occasion. He didn't seize the offer of a dynasty, but seized instead the offer of mercy hidden in God's proposal. He pled for his people.

Moses exhibited selflessness, but he was not a weak leader; he bowed before a holy God, but he could not bend before evil. When apostasy reared its defiant head, he made worshippers of the golden calf drink their god, melted and watered down.

Moses knew exactly who he was and what he stood for. Intensely devoted to the God he met regularly in the Tent of the Presence, Moses could afford to be a servant-ruler. He was the definitive answer to haughty Pharaoh, furiously driving his chariot, leading Egypt's finest toward their doom under the Red Sea.

After Moses we enter a wild and woolly period of the Judges, a time when freelance heroes helped Israel climb into nationhood. They are heroes of a peculiar sort. Gideon's army had to be drastically reduced before he could throw a vast Philistine force into confusion with trumpets and torches. Muscle-bound Samson accomplishes his greatest feat only after being shorn of physical strength, blinded, and led about by a rope. Calling out, "O Sovereign Lord, remember me," he pulled down the temple of his haughty oppressors.

Only humbled heroes can be successful. Centuries later the apostle Paul would put a title on this theme: "God has chosen the weak things of the world to shame the strong."

Saul vs. David

The age of kings arrived for Israel in the person of a Benjamite named Saul, son of Kish. His life is a psychological study in how a man moves from healthy humility to neurotic pride. Chosen for leadership by Samuel, Saul at first submitted to the prophet's guidance. Keenly aware that he came from an insignificant family in one of Israel's smallest tribes, he felt honored. Shortly after his anointing as king, "the spirit came upon him in power," and he began to prophesy.

Saul seemed secure in his role as a servant ruler. Once he led a dramatic rescue operation that freed the town of Jabesh from a besieging Ammorite army. Flushed with victory, his enthusiastic followers remembered some malcontents who had mocked the idea of Saul, this unsophisticated donkey driver, as king. They began shouting, "Bring these men to us and we will put them to death." Enjoying great popularity, Saul had the perfect opportunity to rid himself of potential opposition. But he quickly squelched the idea: "No one shall be put to death today, for this day the Lord has rescued Israel."[1] His focus was on the God who had brought victory.

But somehow that focus changed. Saul veered off on his own course. He stepped into the role of a prophet by making ceremonial burnt offerings in Samuel's place. He disobeyed divine commands against keeping any of the booty won in battles with idolatrous neighbors. Officers barely kept him from having his own son Jonathan executed for disobeying a petty rule.

By the time David the Goliath-slayer came on the scene, Saul's pride was firmly enthroned—and thus continually threatened. He became jealous of David's exploits. Saul spent the rest of his life pursuing this rival, alienating his son, groping in the dark for that lost connection with divine power. Saul would look anywhere for help, even in the mutterings of a spiritualist medium. But he wouldn't look up. He wouldn't bow. God could be anything except bigger than himself.

David offers us a contrasting picture. Though deeply flawed, he knew how to come before God in repentance. This is perhaps the greatest legacy of Israel's greatest king. King David faced his moment of truth when the prophet Nathan walked into his palace and boldly exposed him as an adulterer and murderer. He hadn't been able to cover up the Bathsheba incident completely. But once confronted with the ugly truth, David didn't just eliminate this prophetic irritant, as most monarchs would have done. He humbled himself before his Lord.

David sought mercy with heartfelt eloquence in Psalm 51, clutching the hope that: "a broken and contrite heart,/O God, you will not despise." [2] Later, in Psalm 131, David seemed to have discovered the profound security of the humble:

> My heart is not proud, O Lord,
> my eyes are not haughty;
> I do not concern myself with great matters
> or things too wonderful for me.
> But I have stilled and quieted my soul;
> like a weaned child with its mother,
> like a weaned child is my soul within me. [3]

The bright spots in Israel's history come when kings humble themselves to seek the Lord. The dark streaks come when kings lift up their hearts arrogantly against Him. This essential plot is played out over and over.

When Shishak and his Egyptian army besieged Jerusalem and threatened King Rehoboam, an oppressive tyrant, the light finally broke through: "The leaders of Israel and the king humbled themselves and said, 'The Lord is just.' "[4] As a result, God granted them some measure of deliverance.

After several military successes, King Uzziah of Judah decided to expand his job description. He entered the sacred temple and began to burn incense at the altar. Priests objected. He raged at them and then turned white with leprosy. The chronicler summed him up with words that applied to many others: "After Uzziah became powerful, his pride led to his downfall."[5]

Pride brought disaster, but humility could bring great triumphs. Youthful King Josiah initiated a revival and reformation in Judah that for a time turned the tide against idolatry. God congratulated him—"because your heart was responsive and you humbled yourself before the Lord . . . you tore your robes and wept in my presence."[6]

Humility could rescue even the worst of tyrants. Manasseh did about as much as any man can to destroy morality and decency among his people. But then, while a prisoner of the Assyrians, he "humbled himself greatly before the God of his fathers." Amazingly enough, Manasseh was freed and placed back on his throne. He went on to become a just, reform-minded ruler.

But reforms didn't last. First Israel, then Judah finally slunk off into moral and physical captivity. The epitaph on this period is recorded in the last chapter of 2 Chronicles. Jeremiah was pleading with Zedekiah, the last pathetic king to strut onto the throne of Judah. But he "did not humble himself before Jeremiah the prophet, who spoke the word of the Lord."[7]

In contrast to this disaster, we have the story of Nebuchadnezzar. He is King Saul revisited. Here is a psychological study of someone moving from world-class egotism to the health and wholeness of the humble. First God got the monarch's attention with a prophetic glimpse of his place in the divine plan. Nebuchadnezzar was impressed by God as a "revealer of mysteries." Next God delivered three steadfast Hebrew youths from Nebuchadnezzar's fiery furnace. The king responded by bowing before the heavenly Rescuer.

But still pride lingered. From his palace he could look out over the great temple of Marduk, the seven-storied ziggurat, the hanging gardens. Babylon, which he had built, loomed large, the God of heaven shrunk. Nebuchadnezzar's ego burst out again—and snapped. The ego collapsed in on itself. Nebuchadnezzar became so deranged he would crawl around on all fours and eat grass.

But in the end this king fought his way through pride and managed to look up: "I . . . raised my eyes toward heaven, and my sanity was restored." He had finally had found Someone bigger to admire, from the heart: "I, Nebuchadnezzar, praise and exalt and glorify the King of heaven, because everything he does is right and all his ways are just. And those who walk in pride he is able to humble."[8]

Preparing the Way

Among Israel's prophets, Isaiah became humility's greatest spokesman. His most striking picture comes from a contrast between two larger-than-life figures. Early in his book, as he prophesies against the king of Babylon in chapter 14, Isaiah presents us with Lucifer, "Morning Star." This glorious being wanted to receive adoration from the heavenly assembly and arrive at a position equal to that of the

Most High. After a conflict in heaven, this pompous overachiever was cast down to the earth.

Isaiah's book reaches its peak in chapter 53, where a Suffering Servant appears on the scene, described as a "root out of dry ground," someone without beauty or majesty to make him attractive. There was nothing outwardly desirable about him; he was despised and rejected by men. Here the coming of Christ, the glorious Messiah, is pictured as the antithesis of all kingly splendor. Instead of seizing power He pours out His life unto death, meek as a lamb led dumb before its shearers. Yet it is He who triumphs in the end.

This prophecy sets the stage for the great conflict between Christ and Satan, a three-year duel to be played out in Galilee and Judea, and reveals one of its important themes: pride vs. humility. The two protagonists embody those two qualities to the ultimate degree. Here is the old conflict of Moses and Pharaoh brought to cosmic size. Satan's ego was so grotesquely big it felt cramped even in the peaceful expanse of heaven. Christ compressed His divinity into what men would regard as a zero.

And so the stage was set. The long struggle of humility to shine in a dark, proud land drives us to Bethlehem. It also spotlights the one who prepared the way for the Messiah, John the Baptist. He made a spectacle of himself—out in the desert dressed in camel skins, chewing on locusts and wild honey. His passionate harangues attracted huge crowds. John could easily have built a cult around himself. Instead he pointed elsewhere, to the Lamb of God. And he kept pointing.

When his followers warned that Jesus was drawing all the crowds away, John replied, "A man can receive only what is given him from heaven." He had discovered the contentment of the humble. And then he uttered that well-known battle cry of the humble: "He must become greater; I must become less."[9] John wasn't speaking in resignation. He was talking about his joy, the joy of the bridegroom's friend at the wedding. Jesus was now joined to the people, his chosen bride. "That joy is mine," John said, "and it is now complete." But John's mission remained bigger than himself. He could still enjoy it when it moved past him.

Humility's Definitive Act

The climax of the Bible and the climax of the story of humility comes in the act of God's emptying Himself. It happened when the Almighty decided to enter the world as its Savior. Of all the grand entrances you could imagine for the Lord of the universe, the least likely one would involve a feeding trough in a barn, surrounded by livestock, shepherds, and two peasants. Here the divine identity is so secure as to become almost weightless; the godhood of the man-child is all but invisible. God doesn't need an imposing palace, groveling retinue, silk garments, or trumpets blaring in order to assure Himself that He is royalty. (*I am who I am.*) He can be ignored and still proceed surely toward His destiny. That's light humility.

Jesus traveled light throughout His ministry, a rabbi without credentials or institutional support who ushered in the kingdom of heaven on foot and face-to-face. There never were any trumpets blaring.

When He introduced the nature of His kingdom to a crowd gathered on a hillside by Lake Galilee, His first words blessed the poor in spirit, those who mourn, and the meek.

When adults primed for a mid-life crisis asked Jesus who would be considered the greatest in the kingdom of heaven, He replied, "Whoever humbles himself like this child."[10]

The clash of pride with humility came into sharp focus in Jesus' long-running skirmish with the religious elite of his time. The Pharisee experts in the law looked down on this unlettered Galilean who presumed to teach. They guarded their turf, fiercely proud of their well-defined island of religious goodness. But Jesus expanded the law by focusing on its essentials, speaking on goat trail, in sheep meadow, and by lakeshore with anyone who will listen.

The Sadducees in rich robes and influential positions were also offended by this plain Man who remained on unfriendly terms with privileged Mammon. They couldn't fathom how poverty could possibly be a blessing. He didn't flatter those who could help Him. He kept associating with those who had no status.

The Pharisees and Sadducees just couldn't stoop to acknowledge a greater spiritual power. Jesus would not abandon His utter lack of position. Irreconcilable differences hardened into active enmity. Pride plotted to rid the neighborhood of this unsightly humility that was a constant rebuke. And in the end, the lowly Galilean triumphed by laying Himself out on the killing ground of Golgotha. Pride tried hard to mock, but it soon choked amid the awe-ful echo of an empty tomb.

Chapter Six

WATER SPLASHED IN A BASIN

Having been swept along through Scripture by the epic of humility, we end up pointed squarely at the teaching of the New Testament. That's where the quality is given explicit authority. "Whoever humbles himself like this child," Jesus assured His disciples, "is the greatest in the kingdom of heaven."[1] Peter advised: "Humble yourselves, therefore, under God's mighty hand, that he may lift you up in due time."[2] Paul saw the trait as an essential garment of the believer: "Clothe yourselves with . . . humility."[3]

New Testament teaching also shows us what humility does; it gives that quality a functional shape. And we begin to see that this primary color itself embodies many different hues.

Clearing Away Clutter

First of all, we see it is the Great Purger, cleansing us from a great deal of common clutter so that artful goodness can emerge.

One evening during the Passover season, Jesus' inner circle fell into what they presumed to be an intense theological debate. The disciples began discussing the nature of Christ's kingdom. Surely this was a significant topic worthy of their examination—especially since their

Leader's rather plain statements on the subject seemed to need elaboration. Just how would it be organized, or more specifically, just how would they—its designated heirs—organize it?

No one wanted to compete with Christ as head of state, of course, but what about those nice little vice-presidential slots? You didn't want to be pushy, but, after all, *somebody* had to occupy them. Hints had been dropped that a seat at the right or left hand of the Master in the kingdom would be greatly appreciated.

The disciples talked about all this walking behind Jesus through the streets of Jerusalem toward the Upper Room. That's where thousands of years of Passovers remembered would soon be given a new substance. That night would create a historic crossroads where two covenants met, intertwined for a few moments, and then exchanged the sacred burden of meaning forever. But the disciples couldn't see this coming; they were too involved in hammering out specifics about their relative status.

Who would be greatest in the coming kingdom? Andrew and John could stake claim to being the first to follow Christ, making the transition from followers of John the Baptist to the One pointed out as the "Lamb of God." Peter, the discussion's inevitable leader, might interject that he was first to "really" follow Christ, leaving behind his fishing business once and for all there by the Sea of Galilee. Others could quickly point out that they were called the very same day and also made the decision to become fishers of men. Judas, clearing his throat, could say that one who already carried financial responsibilities for the group merited serious consideration.

Several disciples (if not all) were drawn into the competition. As they put forth their qualifications more and more heatedly, all their hidden jealousies and resentments tumbled out.

By the time these men climbed up the stairs to their rented room, reclined on pillows by the table, kicked off their sandals, and realized that no servant was there to perform the customary chore of washing everyone's feet, not a soul felt like fetching some water. They eyed each other accusingly, wanting someone to blame for the bad feelings each felt guilty about.

Nearby lay the pitcher, basin and towel, accenting the silence. No one moved to touch them.

Jesus had been deep in thought, contemplating the traumatic events to come. But He knew what was on everyone's mind. He felt their alienation. Without a word He rose from His place at the head of the table where wine and bread would shortly embody His divinity, and removed His cloak. The master slowly wrapped a towel around His waist and poured water from pitcher to basin. He moved with deliberation, but not reluctance.

Every eye in the room followed His movements, every ear heard the water splashing, filling the basin. It sounded to them like an ocean.

Jesus then knelt down and washed the streets of Jerusalem from His disciples' feet. He bathed the toes of John, first to come to Him, yes. He cleansed the soles and ankles of Peter, dynamic leader who had sacrificed everything. He washed the feet of Judas, renowned financier, and of Nathaniel, great intellectual, and of Philip who had told Nathaniel about Jesus in the first place, and of James whose mother had first put in a bid for the right-hand position. Jesus washed the feet of all these great luminaries—and the ocean swept over them. They saw who it was draped in a soiled towel. Decades later John would remember with a pang: "Knowing that the Father had given all things into His hands and that He had come forth from God, and was going back to God . . . He poured water into the basin, and began to wash the disciples' feet."[4]

The twelve finally got out of themselves, using the leverage that Christ's masterful humility provided them. Their pretensions were flooded away. This preface to the Last Supper lightened everyone's burden of pride. It wasn't some groaning act of humiliation. It was articulate, light humility. Jesus made a statement; He expressed Himself eloquently. He showed what it means to be human, unencumbered by self-centeredness, and what it means to be God, encumbered with a passion for serving.

Traveling Light

Light humility clears away the clutter. It solves a lot of problems that consistently plague us. We are so easily offended. Little slights at the office and careless remarks at home can emotionally incapacitate us for days. We spend countless hours mulling over the injustice of it all. Defending ourselves takes so much energy. Always having to fend off some threat to our ego can grind us down.

New Testament teaching asks us instead to make a better sacrifice: "Crucify the flesh with its passions and desires." We must take up our own cross; the "old self" must be put to death. This sounds harsh, but we need badly to make a clean break with the baggage of selfishness.

With light humility we don't have to try to untangle the labyrinth of our self; we just move out of it—vacate. Admiring God, centering on God, gives us that kind of leverage. We can crucify the old because we have something immeasurably better to hold on to.

The flip side of casting out the old baggage is finding a more secure identity in Christ. There's nothing like gaining a little perspective, outside the confines of your ego. Those humbled before the Cross, who seek their identity in Someone greater, find it in abundance. Those bowed down are lifted up as the chosen, dearly loved, children of God. They are accepted in the Beloved, without blemish, blessed with every spiritual blessing, a royal priesthood, the salt of the earth, instruments for noble purposes, temples of the living God, trophies led in triumphal procession, having a citizenship in heaven.

The fierceness of the call to be crucified is more than matched by the fervor with which God names the believer. He gives us an identity that nothing can dilute. No misfortune or slander or failure can erase the fact that we are precious in His sight.

Having this, the humble are content. They are promised "all sufficiency in everything" and "an abundance for every good deed." The humble realize that "we brought nothing into the world, and we can take nothing out of it." And so, "if we have food and clothing, we will be content with that." They don't make unconditional demands on life; they travel light. Those still entwined in selfish expectations are always bumping into a world of difficulties; they never quite catch up with all that there is to gripe about. But the people busily admiring the God who cherishes them find fewer and fewer reasons to complain about the rough times.

A promising young Pharisee named Saul clutched a fierce expectation: he thought the world should bow before his orthodoxy, and he was willing to wield the sword against those sects stubborn enough to work against it.

On his way to make holy war against a group of Christians in Damascus, God knocked Saul off his high horse. The persecutor suddenly realized that he had been persecuting the God of heaven. Blinded by this light, he sought out believers in Damascus as a seeker instead of grand inquisitor, and became a follower of Christ.

Saul had occupied a place of privilege in Jewish circles. He had all the accessories of power. He had plenty of props for his ego. But when he came to really admire God, these all become superfluous:

> "A Hebrew of Hebrews; in regard to the law, a Pharisee; as for zeal, persecuting the church; as for legalistic righteousness, faultless. But whatever was to my profit I now consider loss for the sake of Christ. What is more, I consider everything a loss compared to the surpassing greatness of knowing Christ Jesus my Lord, for whose sake I have lost all things. I consider them rubbish, that I may gain Christ and be found in him."[5]

This man traveled light. Completely identified with Someone greater than himself, he became buoyant. He lost his place among society's elite; the Jewish culture that had nurtured this brilliant man now found him to be a scandal. But he had found a bigger place in a more important relationship.

Paul's letters reveal how deeply he'd been changed. This supremely confident man could have become every bit as bigoted in his new faith as he had been in his old. But he didn't just grab onto a new ideology; he grabbed onto a new identity. After his conversion, Paul still was man who could battle for the truth. But he battled very differently. In his devotion to Christ he'd found the leverage to unseat a large ego: "I am crucified with Christ." "Christ is all in all."

You can see this lived out in his letters to the Corinthians. Because of doctrinal disputes in the church at Corinth, some believers had begun to classify themselves as followers of Peter, some as followers of a leader named Apollos, some as followers of Paul. To all of them Paul said, "Is Christ divided? Was Paul crucified for you? Were you baptized into the name of Paul?"[6]

Here Paul remained lightweight. He wouldn't try to beef up his authority. His identification with Someone greater was quick and sure. Secondary allegiances didn't matter in the light of the surpassing greatness of knowing Christ.

Thinking of his past as a persecutor moved Paul to say, "I do not even deserve to be called an apostle." Yet he also expressed a confidence most of us would find intimidating: "Therefore I urge you to imitate me."

Paul didn't try to pretend that all his actions were unworthy; he could calmly acknowledge successes. He may have been "the least of the apostles" but he could add, "By the grace of God I am what I am."[7]

When forced to challenge other leaders because of they were dragging congregations back into legalism, he came up with a mind twister: "If I must boast, I will boast of the things that show my weakness."[8] When others fell into arrogance he asked simply, "What do you have that you did not receive?"

Because this apostle had a secure identity in the One who had chosen him, he could afford a balanced perspective. Was he lauded as a successful evangelist? Well, he planted the "seed," someone else watered it, but it is God who causes people to grow. He consistently discounted his own eloquence in favor of the raw power of the Cross. Saul, the self-righteous bigot, had acquired the grace of light humility.

In Philippi, Paul and Silas were angrily accused of anti-Roman activities by the owners of a fortune-telling slave girl. Paul had just exorcised her and she'd stopped her compulsive babbling. A crowd gathered and threatened these "agitators." By the time magistrates arrived, they had to prevent the mob from pummeling the two to death. But to satisfy the crowd, they had the missionaries stripped and beaten.

Paul and Silas then landed in a dungeon, feet fastened in stocks, backs torn and bloody, hands still twitching from the blows, ears ringing with the chanted threats of the pious pagans. They lay there on the stone and straw until midnight. That's when the two began singing hymns to God. The groaning and yelling in other cells subsided. Prisoners usually make noises in the night to drive away the boredom and despair of its darkest hours. But these sounds were unheard of there. Pickpockets, rapists and subversives listened intently to sweet praise ascending through the damp stone and cold bars.

God was moved too. He responded with an earthquake that knocked everyone's stocks off.

Open-eyed Contentment

Paul and Silas had expressed something bigger than their misfortune, something bigger than their bleeding backs, bigger than their raw ankles. It overshadowed their pain.

Paul was used to traveling light. During his missionary journeys this man would be mobbed, stoned, beaten, flogged and shipwrecked.

He was constantly on the run from his outraged countrymen, from outraged pagans, from thieves and "false brethren." He spoke for his life before angry mobs of all persuasions, before kings and consuls. Often hungry and cold, he had no sure place to lay his head at night and no assurance it would be attached in the morning.

But ringing through all his letters, in and out of jail, is a contagious joy, his exalted run-on sentences are full of glorious truths. He sees a big picture. He is filled up, satisfied: "I know what it is to be in need, and I know what it is to have plenty. I have learned the secret of being content in any and every situation, whether well fed or hungry, whether living in plenty or in want. I can do everything through him who gives me strength." [9]

That's another prize of light humility: profound contentment. This is not because the humble become empty and fatalistically accept whatever happens. They're content because they're so filled up. Identified with a great God, they can absorb a wide range of experiences to good effect. They can live each moment for all it's worth.

An artist can't close her eyes against the world. She has to be open, reactive, sensing the breadth of life. And she talks back. Usually the depth of her expression is determined largely by the breadth of her capacity to experience and understand.

Paul shows us a similar artistry of the spirit. He was not content with his eyes closed, grinning and bearing it. He was content because his eyes were wide open to the big picture. He kept an eye out for the blessings his God might twist out of adversity, for the adventures that might blossom from apparent doom.

Paul created an artful goodness. He was part of a great painting. There was a special meaning behind the lives he and his "fellow-workers" led: "through glory and dishonor, bad report and good report; genuine, yet regarded as imposters; known, yet regarded as unknown, dying, and yet we live on; beaten, and yet not killed; sorrowful, yet always rejoicing; poor, yet making many rich; having nothing, and yet possessing everything." [10]

Light humility. This is the antidote to the pettiness that confines us so often. When we get off dead-center, when we move the stodgy rock of self with its tyrannical expectations and demanding habits, then we're able expand to our boundaries. That's how our lives and our religion enlarge.

Remaining Teachable

Light humility means we travel light; it also produces enlightenment. That's because people who find their identity in a holy God are continually learning from Him. They are Mary sitting at Jesus' feet, choosing the one "necessary" thing. They are the ones who exclaim: "In thy light we see light."

This isn't about casually glancing at God from a distance. A merely theoretical knowledge tends to puff people up. The proud are always throwing out the facts they've acquired as if they were the whole picture. But those who admire God close up can't wrap him up so easily; they see far more than they can grasp. An Albert Einstein spending a lifetime pondering the structure of the universe could speak about the little we know compared to all there is to know. Those with a more casual acquaintance with physics and astronomy are usually quicker to take pride in their absolute opinions.

We must be humble in order to see well. It's hard to be honest with ourselves without light humility. Self-importance always bends us toward self-deception. Only the humble can remain teachable. Secure in the acceptance of an infinite God, they find ever more room in which to grow.

I can't think of a better example of this kind of teachableness than Pastor Glenn Coon. He carried out a fruitful ministry among the many in the Adventist Church stuck in a very small religion.

On one occasion, Pastor Coon received an urgent call from the business manager of an academy who'd been cornered by an irate parent. Glenn jumped into his car and hurried to the school. He walked into the business manager's office to find a woman giving the man the tongue lashing of his life. She was upset over some financial mix-up and just went on and on about how monstrously she'd been treated. Pastor Coon listened to the tirade for a few moments, unable to get a word in. His sympathy for the business manager was growing by the second. So he grabbed onto something called "righteous indignation" and interrupted the woman's accusations with a word to his friend: "Do you know what I would do if I were you? I wouldn't even stay in this room with this woman."

The business manager agreed and the two men walked out the door. They proceeded down a stairway from the second floor to the first. About half-way down, Glenn stopped. As he put it, "The Lord caught up with me." This pastor felt he had condemned the woman and acted contrary to "the gospel of Jesus." He told the business manager, "I made a mistake. I gave you poor counsel."

The man replied, "I think you gave me great advice and I'm going to take it." He began hurrying even faster down the rest of the stairway.

But Glenn called out, "I've made a mistake. I have to return."

Glancing up, the business manager said firmly, "If you go back you're going alone."

Now Glenn was really sorry he'd gotten mixed up in this. He'd condemned this woman, however much she might deserve it, without talking things out and he had to make it right. So he started back up the stairs, the hardest stairs he'd ever had to climb in his life. When he got back up to the manager's office he found the woman had stomped on up to the third floor. Glenn thought for a moment, "Oh, you've done enough now. It isn't necessary to walk up another flight."

Pastor Coon had to pray himself up the long stairway to the third floor, one foot at a time. He finally found the woman holed up in the attic. She cast a glance his way as if to nail him to the wall.

"Sister," Glenn began, "I've come to apologize to you for what I said. I want you to forgive me."

"Well," she shot back, "how sorry are you?"

Glenn kept praying hard. "Sister, I am very sorry," he answered. "And I hope you will forgive me."

The woman wasn't through. Like a cat toying with a mouse it doesn't want to release or quite kill, she whined, "Are you sure? Are you SURE?"

After she'd tossed out a few more sarcastic remarks, Glenn managed to say, "Sister, I don't know what the burden of your heart is. But I know there must be a great burden there. And I know that God can take it away. I am sorry that I have condemned you. I should have been praying for you and helping you to bear your burden. I have come up now to pray for you, and with you. And I wonder if you would let me pray with you now?"

The cat peered at its prey for a few seconds and then replied, "Well, OK, if you're sure you mean it."

Pastor Coon prayed for his adversary and as he prayed something happened: "I felt the warmth of the Holy Spirit. The change was in *me*. I had changed from the spirit of condemnation to one of trying to help someone. And the Lord could do something through me."

After Glenn's heartfelt petition the woman began praying and immediately broke down weeping. The pastor listened to the most wrenching confession he'd ever heard. The woman confessed she was to blame for everything that had happened. She described in detail how and why she was at the bottom of all the trouble. Afterward, Glenn was able to help her to make a new spiritual commitment. [11]

Without light humility, Glenn would have never made it up those stairs. The insulted self would have been too heavy. But in admiration of God's kind of forgiveness, he was inspired to go up, all the way up to the attic.

Light humility results in people who are unencumbered, content, teachable. Admirable qualities to have, but still they can leave us with the impression that this is a rather passive virtue, something tailored more for the hermit than the CEO. The humble and meek do have a reputation for getting walked over on the road through life rather than walking confidently down it. "You first" reflexes are said to leave people standing still.

So it's important to be clear about the difference between a pushover and someone infected with light humility. Light humility gives people a strong identity. They are happily related to a glorious God; they know they are part of His purposes. Pushovers don't know who they are and so usually go with the prevailing flow; they're elbowed this way and that by stronger individuals. They can't say "No" to bad or exploitative people because they are desperately looking for identity in their peers. Dependent for an identity on the shape of others, they make themselves shapeless to fit in.

Pastor Coon was anything but shapeless. He didn't place himself in the cat's paws out of a sense of inadequacy, a need for approval. He didn't apologize to be accepted. He apologized to express God's greatness. He humbled himself before this obnoxious woman from a position of strength, not of weakness. That gave him leverage. Those who flop down as doormats because they lack backbone have no leverage; they're simply walked over. But those who become meek as a deliberate expression of God Almighty's grace are a show of force. They may not always be successful. They may be ignored. But their statement still stands; meaningful because God is meaningful. They are artists of the Spirit; they are continually rejuvenated by what their artful goodness expresses.

Chapter Seven

DESERT DWELLERS AND LIVELY SAINTS

The Bible shows us light humility as a grand theme, something worthy of our best energies, something that's part of the big picture. It also gives that quality a specific shape—especially in New Testament teaching. The Christian church down through the ages has tried to express the ethic of humility in a variety of ways. It has created a legacy. Just as in art there are different schools—classical, romantic, realist, impressionist—which contemporary artists look back on and react to, so believers have a tradition of goodness to reflect on.

Adventists have always seen themselves as playing a key end-time role in the history of the church. We believe that God's truth has been progressively revealed, or at least progressively understood. Historic revivals and reformations have illuminated more and more of God's plan for humanity. Europe's great Reformation of the sixteenth century recovered the lost doctrine of justification by faith. The Great Awakening of the eighteenth century in New England recovered the neglected truth of sanctification by faith.

Our desire is to become the culmination of that process. We believe we have absorbed the truths others re-discovered; we stand on their shoulders. And we've also re-discovered other doctrines. In fact, we claim that

Adventist doctrine puts the whole biblical picture together in a system of "present truth." This truth points us all the way to the Second Coming and helps people prepare for that great event.

It's my conviction that there is another dimension to this historic process. Seeing more and more light, thinking straight about God and his plan of salvation, is one important dimension. Living out that light in a way that shows Christ's graces to the world is another. If there is a climax of truth, there is also a climax of virtue. If there is light for the mind, there is also light for the heart.

Unfortunately in the Adventist Church, this lofty pursuit of genuine heart religion ran into a detour. It bogged down in endless debates over "sinless perfection." It lost momentum in the religion of avoidance. Many Adventists fell into the trap of simply trying to be less and less worldly, trying to remove more and more bad things out of their lives. (I discussed this at length in my previous book, *Burned Out on Being Good*.)

When the goal is to be sinless, then sin remains at the center of attention. You're always staring it down, trying to get rid of it. And of course the easiest sins to get rid of are the external ones, the trappings of worldliness. Religion becomes smaller and smaller as it focuses on ever more petty things to get rid of.

The religion of avoidance is anything but an inspiring climax to history. It's a detour, a dead end. We need a very different kind of religion: a religion of qualities. That's what we need to focus on. Our religion can expand greatly when it centers on character qualities, qualities that are as luminous as art, qualities that express something wonderful about our wonderful God.

So let's take a look at this one quality, humility, down through the ages. We stand at the end of a long tradition of believers seeking a religion of the heart. We need to learn from those who have gone before us. It's useful to get our bearings in the history of virtue. That can help us say something more eloquent in the present world and to progress beyond what has gone before.

How can we bring this story to a climax? How can we be part of the big picture at the end of history? That's our challenge today.

Like Corpses

The story of humility in the church is a story of how believers have related to the self. It's both a disturbing and inspiring tale. Some of the first highlights we pick up in ecclesiastical history show us believers attacking the self with revolutionary fervor. Some of the most revered early saints exiled themselves in desert hideaways to pray and abuse their bodies. [1]

Simon Stylites, born in 389, made a spectacle of his humility. As a novice, he tied a rope around his waist so tightly that it cut a deep gash and could scarcely be removed. His abbot dismissed him and warned others about this dangerous maverick. But Simon's fame only grew.

He took to fasting for the whole forty days of Lent, once chaining himself to a rock and standing for days at a time in furious prayer. But he could never get enough self-punishment. Pillar dwelling was a fad among hermits at the time, so Simon constructed one five yards off the ground and lived on it four years. Pillar after pillar followed, built by enthusiastic disciples, each one a bit higher than the last. Finally Simon got himself 60 feet in the air on a six-foot-wide platform. He resided there for 40 years, dressed in animal skins, taking charity from pilgrims and haranguing them about usury, injustice and "the horrible custom of swearing." In between sermons he bobbed about a great deal, kneeling and genuflecting repeatedly in a frenzy.

Simon and other desert dwellers were celebrities, not ordinary believers. But their ideal of mortifying the flesh pervaded the early church. Tertullian tells us: "Christian sinners spend the day sorrowing, and the night in vigils and tears, lying on the ground among clinging ashes, tossing in rough sackcloth and dirt, fasting and praying." He recalled that a penitent adulterer was "led into the midst of the brethren and prostrated, all in sackcloth and ashes . . . a compound of disgrace and horror, before the widows, the elders, suing for everyone's tears, licking their footprints, clasping their very knees. . . ."

Often, the more religious a person, the more he or she engaged in total war against the self. A devout woman named Paula founded a monastic community in Palestine where nuns were advised to pay little attention to dress: "A clean body and clean clothes betoken an unclean mind." She preferred to sleep on the ground and never took a bath unless dangerously ill.

In medieval times this dark picture of humility only became more elaborate. The theologian Bonaventure applauded anyone who was "aroused to insult his own body out of true self-contempt," anyone thus "inflamed with the spirit of true humility." [2] Making a spectacle of one's humility, shouldering it in public, was considered quite a virtue. The disciples of Loyola traveled Europe begging for alms and seeking to do good; many had renounced their eminent learning and influential positions. Once three were offered beds for the night at a hospital. The sheets were filthy and spotted with the blood of recently deceased patients. Two of the men jumped right in. The third, horrified, sought a cleaner place to lay down.

But the next day he felt terrible for his moment of weakness in the battle against self. He wanted badly a chance to redeem his shameful act. At the next village hospital, only one bed was available. Its bedcovers were full of lice from its last occupant, a corpse. The repentant father quickly removed his clothes and slid between the sheets. Lice pinched and stung him all night, making his body smart until it sweated, but he had won "the victory," and his deed would go down in Jesuit history as an act of honor.

Acts like these are removed some distance from Paul, who learned contentment in all circumstances. Here people are seeking the most disagreeable circumstances in order to spite their egos. And in the process the self is again made the center—as the thing constantly and deliberately despised.

The cult of total humility included a belief in total passivity. St. Francis took this view to its logical conclusion. When asked to describe a truly obedient person he proposed a dead body as the best example:

> "Take a corpse and put it where you will! You will see that it does not resist being moved, nor murmur about its position nor protest when it is cast aside. If it is placed on a throne, it will not raise its eyes up, but cast them down. If it is clothed in purple, it will look twice as pale. This is a truly obedient man." [3]

Ignatius of Loyola echoed these sentiments. Men in his Society of Jesus, he wrote, "ought to be like a corpse, which has neither will nor understanding; or like a little crucifix which is turned about at the will of him who holds it." [3]

Full-Color Devotion

In contrast to these pious corpses stands a Carmelite sister named Teresa of Avila. She gives us a pleasant picture of a whole human being

supremely devoted to Jesus. Teresa's mystical nature led her into ec-
static visions of a beautiful, fiery Christ who ravished her with His love.
But she proved to be much more than a contemplative. Teresa took on
the task of reforming her Carmelite order of nuns in the 1560s. The convent in Avila had become a social center for women who wanted an easy,
sheltered life with few responsibilities.

Creating a new order of Carmelites dedicated to a more devotional
and service-oriented life proved to be very hard work. Her reforms
brought on violent opposition from comfortable fellow nuns, a suspicious
nobility, nervous magistrates, and the aroused citizens of Avila who feared
the order might become a financial burden. Teresa endured a great deal
of slander and some outright persecution, but her calmness and consistent spirit of devotion began to win her admirers. With deep roots in her
Redeemer, this sister was secure enough to put criticism to good use.
After one particularly vicious attack, a friend asked how she could hold
her peace. "No music is so pleasing to my ears," she answered with a
grin. "They have reason for what they say, and speak the truth." [4]

Teresa wanted nothing more than to simply live out a quietly useful
life admiring God. She would later look back on her first experiment in
reform with great fondness: "I there enjoyed the tranquillity and calmness which my soul has often since longed for. . . . His divine Majesty
sent us what was necessary without asking, and if at any time we were in
want (which was very seldom) the joy of these holy souls was so much
the greater."

Teresa demonstrated such skill in leading her nuns that she was
asked to help in reforming other orders. Once church officials made her
prioress of a convent that they thought distastefully lax. Teresa had to
take charge of sisters who had no intention of obeying her stricter rules.
Some even became hysterical at the idea of a more disciplined, contemplative life. But Teresa managed to win them over, saying that she'd come
not to coerce or instruct but to serve and learn from the least among
them.

Teresa was that most unusual saintly commodity: a reformer with a
sense of humor. The sisters under her care saw a woman of sweet tem-
perament, affectionately tender towards them, always able to maneuver
them through difficulties with her lively wit and fertile imagination. Teresa
made all their burdens seem light.

This sister lived what most of us would consider a very narrow, cloistered life, but she managed to create a balanced, full-color portrait of devotion. She was an earnest soul seeking only to be lost in Christ, but she could stand up if need be to the highest civil and ecclesiastical authorities of her time. She was a very individualistic mystic constructing her own "Interior Castle," but she willingly submitted all her writings to the judgment of her confessor.

Teresa remained on intimate terms with the One who made her complete. After receiving communion on her deathbed, she exclaimed, "O my Lord, now is the time that we may see each other!"

Both in medieval times and earlier there were others, too, who found themselves rather than abused themselves in Christ. Augustine gives us a sense of his profound satisfaction in the fullness of God. He wrote in his Confessions:

> The enticements of the wanton claim the name of love; and yet nothing is more enticing than thy love, nor is anything loved more healthfully than thy truth, bright and beautiful above all . . . no being has true simplicity like thine, and none is innocent as thou art . . . what sure rest is there save in the Lord? . . . thou art the fullness and unfailing abundance of unfading joy . . . who can deprive thee of what thou lovest? Where, really, is there unshaken security save with thee? [5]

In Thomas A. Kempis we get another glimpse of that profound satisfaction of a human being enjoying the Complete God:

> Trusting in Thy goodness and great mercy, O Lord, I draw near, the sick to the Healer, the hungering and thirsting to the Fountain of life, the poverty-stricken to the King of heaven, the servant to the Lord, the creature to the Creator, the desolate to my own gentle Comforter. [6]

Nicholas of Cusa, writing in his "Vision of God" had a similar perspective, "Thou uncoverest the fountain whence floweth all that is desirable alike in nature and art."

Catherine of Siena understood herself as one of the creatures God had made "most lovingly" in His own image and likeness. Relating her experience in the third person, she wrote:

Obeying His word, she looked into the abyss of charity, and there saw how He was the sovereign and eternal Goodness, how for love He created and then redeemed us by the blood of His Son, and how this same love was the source of all His many gifts to us, whether sufferings or joys. All comes from love, and all God does is ordered toward the salvation of mankind. [7]

Everything for Love

From the Reformation on, the self ceased to be as dramatically abused as in earlier ages. Protestants, at least, no longer believed they could gain merit from deliberate suffering. But many still regarded the self as something "totally depraved," a hotbed of carnality where you could relax only at eternal peril. Believers in general had a better grasp of the basis of salvation. But, as far as relating to oneself, the dominant theme often remained a wearying war against sin.

Still, there were men like Blaise Pascal. He pushed through his chronic, painful illness to a contemplation of God, getting far beyond himself and into an intense enjoyment of the infinite. And there were women like Julian of Norwich who advised fellow-believers:

It is quicker for us and easier to come to the knowledge of God than it is to know our own soul. For our soul is so deeply grounded in God and so endlessly treasured that we cannot come to knowledge of it until we first have knowledge of God, who is the Creator to whom it is united. [8]

A seventeenth century Carmelite lay brother named Lawrence gave the world an unforgettable picture of existing completely toward God. He lived a consistent life of quiet service and seemed to his contemporaries a phenomenon of unbreakable joy. They wanted to know his secret. He once explained:

It is not necessary to have great things to do. I turn my little omelette in the pan for the love of God; when it is finished, if I have nothing to do, I prostrate myself on the ground and adore God, Who gave me the grace to make it, after which I arise, more content than a king. When I cannot do anything else, it is enough for me to have lifted a straw from the earth for the love of God. [9]

What mattered to Lawrence was simply being able to express something wonderful with all his actions. That made the most unglamorous thing a potential work of art. He noted that many believers were trying all kinds of spiritual techniques to get themselves in the presence of God. Lawrence asked:

> Is it not much shorter and more direct to do everything for the love of God, to make use of all the labors of one's state in life to show Him that love, and to maintain His presence within us by this communion of our hearts with His? There is no finesse about it; one has only to do it generously and simply. [9]

Lawrence was spiritually intense, but he bore no wearying burdens. Whenever he sinned he confessed: "I can do nothing better without You. Please keep me from falling and correct the mistakes I make." Then he proceeded on his way without guilty introspection.

As he lay dying at the age of 80, Lawrence was given a few moments alone. When his friends returned to his bedside, they asked how he'd spent the time. He replied that he'd been doing just what he'd be doing for all eternity: "Blessing God, praising God, adoring Him, and loving Him with all my heart."

Other devout men and women of the time were dominated by a very different type of reflection. Some in the Puritan and Reformed tradition turned self-examination into an endlessly depressing exercise. Never quite assured that they were among the chosen of God, they constantly searched for evidences of election to that mysteriously select group. A righteous life obviously was a key. Enthusiastic transports also seemed to point to genuine conversion. But then religious rapture, especially if it got too intense, could be attributed to the Devil. And of course if a person sunk too low after such experiences, as often happened, that also appeared to be the work of the enemy of souls.

The sober Christians who subscribed to this type of Calvinism probably seemed quite humble. But worry over the state of their souls overshadowed any admiration for the God who loved and accepted them.

However, other individuals in that same tradition managed to produce quite different canvases, dominated by the light of admiration. The Puritan divine Richard Baxter wrote this exhortation to believers:

> Love as much as thou canst, thou shalt be ten thousand times more beloved. Dost thou think thou canst over-love Him? What! love more than Love itself?. . . Is it a small thing in thine eyes to be beloved of God?. . . Christian, believe this and think on it. Thou shalt be eternally embraced in the arms of that love, which was from everlasting, and will extend to everlasting. [10]

The great revivalist George Whitefield shows us a man keenly aware of God's gracious acts around him, rather than obsessed with his own frailty. You sense continually that in his journal entries. "How sweetly does Providence order things for us!" he wrote. "Oh may I constantly follow it as the Wise Men did the star in the East." [10]

Nineteenth century Anglican chaplain Forbes Robinson wrote in a letter: "It is glorious to be made in His image, and to be sure that all one's highest yearnings are a reflection—however broken, partial and unsightly—of His own marvelous life. We have indeed cause to be grateful for our 'creation.' "[11]

Resting in the Joy

Hudson Taylor represented a style of Christianity based in the "holiness movement," a style which took "resting in the Lord" and depending completely on him as a primary objective. These believers sought to become cleansed and emptied vessels into which God could pour his Spirit. Taylor in particular championed "the exchanged life," a full identification with Christ, exchanging one's will for His.

You might expect someone with these ideals to become a passive wimp. Taylor was anything but that. He boldly walked into innermost China in 1854 and took on the challenge of evangelizing its unreached millions, who were deeply suspicious of all "foreign devils." Through his faith venture, the China Inland Mission, Taylor almost singlehandedly brought about a revolution in modern missions.

Taylor's exchanged life made him quite adaptable. He wore Chinese clothes, ate Chinese food, and adopted Chinese customs as far as possible—things many other missionaries of the time thought scandalous. But Taylor wanted to raise up a Chinese church free of foreign accessories, a church led by Chinese pastors worshipping in a "thoroughly native style of architecture." And so this man gave himself up to a great goal: "to plant the standard of the Cross in the eleven provinces of China hitherto unoccupied."

The way in which Taylor identified himself with Christ and tried to consciously depend on him for every aspect of his work—from finances to physical survival—moved him to accomplish more, not less. He once wrote: "How many estimate difficulties in the light of their own resources, and thus attempt little and often fail in the little they attempt! All God's giants have been weak men, who did great things for God because they reckoned on His being with them." [12]

Taylor reckoned on that even in the worst of times. When riots broke out against two of the mission stations, a colleague found Taylor softly whistling his favorite hymn: "Jesus, I am resting, resting, in the joy of what Thou art." During many such emergencies, friends came to marvel at his calm courage under pressure.

"Resting in Christ" did not empty Hudson Taylor as a human being. It led to a grand quest that gave meaning to his life. In one letter he wrote: "I cannot tell you how glad my heart is to see the work extending and consolidating in the remote parts of China. It is worth living for and worth dying for."

Taylor had met something bigger than himself. His life was centered, not leveled. That became apparent to a young visitor at Mission headquarters who was quite unimpressed with Taylor's appearance and bearing until he heard the man pray. "I had never heard anyone pray like that," the guest recalled. "There was a simplicity, a tenderness, a boldness, a power that hushed and subdued one . . . he spoke with God face to face. . . ."

Uneasy Truce

In more contemporary times most Christians seem to have developed a modified mixture of what has preceded us. Religious folk are basically mild; we laugh a little, cry a little, have fun a little, worship a little—nothing too extravagant. We've called a truce in the all-out war against the self, but don't know quite what to do with it. The old battles have faded, but we're having a hard time finding a burning center for our lives.

However some do find a wholehearted relationship with a God they can admire, and slip gracefully into light humility. Harry Blamires remembers his literature tutor in the 1930s, the Oxford don C.S. Lewis, in this light. In their book-lined chambers, Oxford dons existed to pursue the scholarly life, not primarily to teach. Students tried to pick up whatever crumbs might fall to them by tagging along behind the tutor wrapped up in his own intellectual pursuits. Many dons, in fact, were notoriously lax, practicing golf strokes on the carpet or catching up on correspondence while the student read his essay to the furniture.

But Lewis, Blamires recalls, "discharged his teaching obligations with punctilious care and thoroughness." Students learned from someone who showed consideration, not someone looking down on them from his considerable accomplishments in English literature. Whenever Lewis needed to point out a serious flaw in some essay, he would try to combine it with praise for some other virtue in the piece.

Humility enabled Lewis to teach well. He had no memorized lines about how unworthy he was; he didn't pursue humiliation. He lived as a respected intellectual. But he did bow wholeheartedly and with his whole mind before the holy God of Scripture. You can sense a light humility in the pleasure Lewis took in pointing out George MacDonald as the inspiration for much of his allegories, and in his warm praise for his contemporary Christian writer G. K. Chesterton.

Lewis could also enjoy his own successes as much as those of others. Blamires remembers him digging out the French edition of "The Lion, the Witch, and the Wardrobe," and delightedly pointing out how the French illustrator had captured a facet of his mythical characters different from that created by the English artist. Lewis took special pleasure in the praise the Narnia chronicles gathered from a very wide audience. All this served to deepen his gratitude.

Blamires makes special note of Lewis's quality of contentment. After referring to Lewis's rather demanding mother and alcoholic brother, Blamires writes:

> What an astonishing man he was at putting up with things! Childhood in Ireland, schooldays in England, war service in France were all marked at times by miseries which many a literary man would have turned into material for agonizing protest fiction. Yet how rarely is the note of grievance heard in Lewis' output! His own griefs and trials were mentioned only when mentioning them

might help someone else to bear theirs. [13]

C. S. Lewis is the man of our age who perhaps best exhibits for me the winsomeness of light humility. In fact it was reading his thoughts on the subject in "The Screwtape Letters" some years ago which started me on the trail of that quality.

In my search I've discovered that the humility coming to us from Scripture is not some flat leveling of the soul but a great collision of two enormous facts: The self must be killed, and the self must be cherished in Christ. Both facts are powerful and neither can be watered down. "We have this treasure in jars of clay."

Those men abusing themselves in the desert were trying to express something important: crucify the self. Their harsh strokes on the canvas are something to remember. But we must add the other colors as well, God's assurances of our infinite value in His eyes. Both are needed to fill out the picture; we don't want to fall into the old trap of dark humility, but neither do we want to settle for some airhead grace that takes God's benediction without looking at its cost.

Today the pendulum may have swung too far away from those ancient saints mortifying the flesh. The cult of indulgence has certainly wiped out any remains of the cult of suffering. We're properly embarrassed now by forefathers unable to enjoy life's pleasures. But perhaps we've lost their sense of a high and holy calling as well.

How can we express our admiration for the Sovereign God today? That's part of our calling as believers. That's part of our calling as Adventists.

Light humility is a quality that expands our lives. It makes of our lives a bigger picture that reflects our big picture of God. We have something to remember: the winsomeness of Teresa, the cheerful service of Lawrence, the dedication of Hudson Taylor, the graciousness of C.S. Lewis. This is a tradition we have to build on. How can we take it to new heights?

It's not a matter of quantity; it's not a matter of doing a greater amount of things to make ourselves humble. It's a matter of quality. Only qualities can express what God is like. Only qualities create artful goodness.

What new form can we give in our world to this invisible virtue? In the details of our everyday life we can make brush strokes on a great canvas, our contentment and teachability and graciousness can add to the picture, the wonderful big picture of what God is really like.

Chapter Eight

THE SHIELD WE MUST DEFEND

The concept of honor is one of humanity's most fascinating guiding lights. For centuries people have behaved in certain ways in order to preserve this very valuable thing—their honor. The idea in the West probably started among Indo-European tribes working out their hierarchies in the forests, determining who belonged among the worthy and who did not. They created a primal honor of the strongest, the bravest, the most fertile. Being kinless or "ill-born" always excluded a person from the ranks of the honorable; the deformed were looked upon as God-cursed. An old French peasant proverb said: "There is more pity shown to a clod than to an orphan."

Honor is how people have tried to achieve self-worth in relation to others. Norfolk in Richard II declared: "Mine honour is my life . . . Take honour from me, and my life is done." The Roman Antony put it more succinctly: "If I lose mine honour, I lose myself."

Honor flowered in the age of chivalry when knights developed their own special code. They engaged in tournaments and fought battles and wooed ladies in a certain way in order to "win glory before death." Military action was regarded as morally purifying. The Norse hero Beowulf tells King Hrothgar, "Better is it for each one of us that he should avenge his friend, than greatly mourn."

Reputation mattered above all else, even a posthumous one. Xenophon defended the glory of warriors in this way: "And when their fated end comes, they do not lie forgotten and without honor, but they are remembered and flourish eternally in men's praises."[1]

The medieval church shaped this warrior ideal into the Christian knight who defends the faith, or goes on an epic quest in pursuit of the holy grail. Knights could be turned into crusaders by appealing to their honor. Those Moslems in Palestine, those unclean heathen, had insulted them by taking over and defiling their sacred cites; red-blooded Christians must respond.

The traditional sense of honor always goes back to warrior ideals. In 1811, John Randolph cautioned Americans against fighting the British. John C. Calhoun made this passionate reply: "Sir, I here enter my solemn protest against this low and 'calculating avarice' entering this hall of legislation." Peace with submission, he declared, was "only fit for shops and countinghouses . . . [the nation] is never safe but under the shield of honor."[2]

Traditional honor is always about defining and maintaining your position before others. It's wrapped up in titles and uniforms. It's supposed to protect you in some way; but you're always having to prop it up. It remains something of a paradox: the shield we must defend. You must always be on the lookout for insults and slights. Men resort to duels in order defend their honor, absolving their good name even at the cost of killing someone.

In order to maintain your place of honor in society you're always looking for someone to dishonor. The elite usually distinguish themselves by rejecting the lowly, the alien, the shamed.

Shame, not guilt, was the great fear in cultures that put a premium on honor. A woman could be socially destroyed by rape, even though she was morally guiltless. It was the shame that proved unbearable and doomed "soiled" women to social isolation.

At the same time, men might carry on private affairs and still cash in on their honor. It was only if adultery became a public scandal that shame entered the picture and threatened their position.

Too Proud to Sin

In the recent past, honor has served as the secular way to be good. People hope that their honor will keep them from shameful sins. And that ideal has probably helped for some time to keep gross immorality at bay. But it tends to break down when the heat is on. After all, if honor is a possession I'm defending, then it shouldn't make too many demands on me. It can't stand over me; it can't call me to higher moral ground.

A woman is traditionally supposed to "defend her honor" if tempted by a seducer. But when there's little shame attached to giving in, there's little threat to honor. It's easy to give up on that possession anyway. Virtue centered around personal honor boils down to a hope that we'll be too proud to commit certain sins. But of course temptation makes it very easy to be humble.

Traditional honor also changes shape—depending on whatever group is bestowing it.

Take the honor of West Point graduates, for example. A West Point "master of the sword" declared, "Here in everything we do, we talk of honor." Cadets must live by a code of honor, pledging, "I will not lie, cheat, or steal, nor tolerate those who do." That ethic reinforced the unity of this uniformed, titled elite. [3]

West Point promotes some very healthy virtues. But out in the battlefield the pressures of the group are different. Senior military leaders, many of whom were West Point graduates, became infamous for their inflated "body counts" in Vietnam. Deception became part of the honor of the group.

Traditional honor doesn't hold up well when the heat is on. Principally because it's soft; it bends with whatever principles your group reinforces at the moment. Honor as a possession we must defend often dissolves into bigotry and vengeance.

Traditional honor has obvious liabilities. And yet, we all sense a basic need to act honorably. We long to be part of something honorable. Human life has a grander shape when we're aiming at ideals. We need a noble structure for our lives; we need meaning. Just doing whatever feels right at the moment doesn't take us very far. It leaves us constantly trying to find out who we are.

This is our dilemma. We can't go back to the old honor of shields and titles and coats of arms. We don't want to just exclude the lowly in order to be included with the noble. And yet we long for something that will hold us together, something that will guide us in our relationships with others.

Can we have a human life without honor? Can we find an honor that doesn't war against human life?

Adventists are facing this dilemma in our own unique way. The old marks that distinguished us as a special people, a remnant people, are slowly disappearing. We used to be able to find a secure identity in a distinctive style—the way we dressed, the things we ate, the music we listened to, the amusements we avoided. We had our own schools and hospitals and publishing houses, even our own language.

Our religion was a shield that not only protected us from the world but assured us that we were much better than the world. We were proud to be Seventh-day Adventists.

Well, now that Adventist uniform is fading. We don't look that different from people "in the world." It's not so easy to tell us apart. We're more mainstream. Our institutions are trying to build bridges instead of walls.

And many ache in the absence of those old "landmarks." It's good to be able to relate to "non-Adventists" in a more winsome way. It's good to move beyond legalistic externals. But what about having a meaningful shape for our lives? What about ideals that will guide us in our relationships?

Can we recapture the ethic of honor in a way that will expand us instead of constrict us? Can we find an honor that won't make our religion too small?

Look, Simply Look

We find an answer in something remarkable that happened in 19th century London. Victorian England was one of the clearest examples of a society based on honor. In that very class-conscious world, the old warrior honor had matured into middle-class respectability. Basic decency could be expected of gentlemen. Moral scandal was to be avoided.

This wasn't bad. But the frailties of traditional honor were also apparent. The good citizens of London, for example, preserved their good name primarily by avoidance. They avoided sexual suggestiveness of course, but they also avoided crudeness in general—and that included vast numbers of the population: the lower classes.

Soberly dressed ladies and gentlemen promenading London's

streets in elegant carriages politely turned their gaze from the filthy, illiterate urchins on the streets. They generally considered it bad taste to discuss the miseries of those beneath them.

The Industrial Revolution was wooing multitudes from farm to factory, where machines promised regular wages but demanded twelve hour-a-day drudgery. The destitute could apply to workhouses for refuge, but conditions there were kept so bad that all who could move their bodies fled to work of any kind.

As usual, the children of the poor suffered most. In a prospering, relatively enlightened land their options were pitifully limited. Many were worked to death in factories. Many had to flee homes where desperate straits bred alcoholism, prostitution, and deadly epidemics. And these homeless children created the world Charles Dickens would expose—orphanages where they subsisted under the stern rule of their betters, or the mean streets where petty crime could keep them alive a few more days.

These people were without honor. They had no social place, no leverage. And the honor of their superiors erected a barrier to keep them in their tragic underworld.

Charles Haddon Spurgeon grew up in this society as a typical middle-class Victorian from a respectable family. He was a good boy who liked to study. His brother James recalled, "I kept rabbits, chickens, and pigs and a horse; he kept to books." At the age of fifteen, Charles had become familiar with the Puritan theologians.

This deeply sensitive lad began to wrestle with the problem of sin and guilt. The "universal requirements of God's law" weighed on him night and day. He knew he had committed transgressions against Almighty God. He was lost; what could he do about it?

Charles visited church after church, trying to get a clear answer: "One man preached Divine sovereignty, but what was that sublime truth to a poor sinner who wished to know what he must do to be saved. There was another admirable man who always preached about the law, but what was the use of ploughing up ground that needed to be sown. Another was a practical preacher . . . but it was very much like a commanding officer teaching the maneuvers of war to a set of men without feet . . . what I wanted to know was 'How can I get my sins forgiven?' and they never told me that." [4]

One Sunday a snowstorm drove Charles into a small Primitive

Methodist church where a layman was preaching. This obviously un-lettered man stumbled through a talk on one text: "Look unto me, and be ye saved." He explained, "Now lookin' don't take a deal of pain. It ain't liftin' your foot or your finger; it is just 'Look.' "

Charles saw a glimmer of hope in the crude exposition. The speaker proclaimed a Christ who said, "Look unto Me; I am sweatin' great drops of blood. Look unto Me; I am hangin' on the cross." The man kept hammering away at his point that we must look, simply look.

And suddenly the mystery was unlocked for Charles. He had been longing to do fifty things to gain salvation—make a pilgrimage, scourge himself, anything that might give him assurance—but here he discovered the one single act that mattered: looking at Jesus on the cross in faith. It struck Charles as a revelation: "I could have risen that instant, and sung with the most enthusiastic of them, of the precious blood of Christ, and the simple faith which looks alone to Him." The revelation sank in: "I was an emancipated soul, an heir of heaven, a forgiven one, accepted in Jesus Christ, plucked out of the miry clay and out of the horrible pit . . ."

Charles was overwhelmed by the realization that God did not look at him as he was, a convicted sinner, but as someone emancipated, accepted in Jesus. This good news broke over him with great power. It was to become the central theme in his long ministry in London as the "Prince of Preachers."

The evangelical gospel shaped Charles Spurgeon's theology and gave him a burning mission. Interestingly enough, it also enabled him to become something more than a typical Victorian gentleman. He could not, for example, pass off the wretchedness of the lower classes as something beneath him, something inevitable. He saw every human being as an object of God's grace.

A Right to Grace

A look at Spurgeon's many-faceted ministry at the Metropolitan Tabernacle shows us just how seriously he took that grace. The Tabernacle constantly bulged with activity—volunteers sewing clothes for the children at the orphanage, preparing bouquets for the sick, and learning how to help expectant mothers. Others busied themselves with the Blind Society, the Female Servants' Home Society, the Gospel Temperance Society, the Loan Building Fund, the Christian Brothers' Benefit Society, and the Spurgeon's Sermons Tract Society. Still other Tabernacle members went out to minister to the destitute in some 40 missions scattered around South London, teaching street children at "Ragged Schools," and selling inexpensive books and pamphlets to the population. Spurgeon's gospel-driven energy inspired Tabernacle members to move beyond occasional acts of conventional charity. They created an energetic body of grace that helped to transform the wretched.

Spurgeon built an orphanage very different from the institutions that children like Oliver Twist endured. He determined to avoid barrack-like quarters, uniforms and everything else that reminded kids they were objects of charity. Spurgeon had individual homes built, each one with a name, each one with a matron acting as mother to 14 boys or girls. He built a gymnasium and swimming pool. The homes formed a quadrangle enclosing a grassy playing field broken up with flowers and shrubs where children who'd been cramped in filthy hovels and narrow streets could expand their lives.

Whenever Spurgeon dropped by, the children thronged around him. He made it a point to know all their names and to have a penny for each one. These children from a variety of backgrounds—black and white, Jew and Gentile, Anglican and Catholic—mingled in a healthy atmosphere, all objects not of pity, but of grace, all redeemable.

Spurgeon also tried to help their older brothers, many unemployed or working long hours for pitiful wages. Without education they had virtually no chance of improving their lives. So the pastor organized evening classes at the tabernacle where young men could study free of charge. He also enabled a great many impoverished young men to get through his Pastor's College.

Since the biggest event in Spurgeon's life was the day grace came to him—the undeserving—he knew how to give graciously. When he noticed that one student's clothes were badly worn, he stopped the young man and asked him to go on an errand. He was to deliver a note to a certain address and wait for the reply. The address turned out to be a tailor's shop and the message required the tailor to supply a new suit and coat for the boy.

Spurgeon didn't just ignore class differences; he rammed his fist through them. He also battled larger prejudices. When Indian nationalists led a small revolt against British rule and were mowed down, Spurgeon called for a service of national humiliation. This was a time when Englishmen boasted of India as the jewel of their vast Empire on which the sun never set. Imperialism would not become a bad word until the next century. But Spurgeon spoke on behalf of the Indian people against the actions of his government, reminding all that "only righteousness could exalt a nation," and then he took up an offering to assist those wounded in the revolt.

On another occasion, Spurgeon met a black man who'd escaped from slavery in South Carolina and asked him to talk about his experiences at an evening Tabernacle service. This brought strong criticism from America, which was then heading toward Civil War. Many American Christians, who'd become avid readers of his sermons, demanded that he state his position on the matter clearly. Spurgeon did: "I do from my inmost soul detest slavery . . . and although I commune at the Lord's table with men of all creeds, yet with a slave-holder I have no fellowship. . . . Whenever one has called upon me, I have considered it my duty to express my detestation of his wickedness."

From Noun to Verb

For Spurgeon, every human being had a right to the grace that had overwhelmed him in his darkest hour. No man could be declared beneath redemption, whether Indian revolutionary or black slave or street urchin. All must be regarded in the light of the cross. In this remarkable man and his London ministry one sees that old noun honor—encrusted with knightly coats-of-arms, hoary with clannish loyalties, propped up as respectability—suddenly become a verb, a powerful verb. Spurgeon escaped the confines of conventional honor by honoring.

And in his honor we find artful goodness. He created a wonderful canvas set against the somber hues and dignified patterns of Victorian England. Grace erupted like a flood of red and yellow all over the grim slums of South London. Huddled under an endless factory smoke haze, gray human lives blossomed into bright colors.

Spurgeon's humor had a special place in the composition. He was a great orator who drew huge crowds into the Metropolitan Tabernacle, but he managed to side-step the stuffy propriety of most clergymen. In the midst of one of his dead-serious lessons on preaching at the Pastor's College, Spurgeon could launch into side-splitting comedy. A student recalled:

> Then came those wonderful imitations of the dear brethren's peculiar mannerisms; one with the hot dumpling in his mouth, trying to speak; another sweeping his hand up and down from nose to knee; a third with his hands under his coat-tails, making the figure of a water-wagtail. . . . By this means he held the mirror before us so that we could see our faults, yet all the while we were almost convulsed with laughter. He administered the medicine in effervescing draughts.

Enveloped in rock-solid grace, Spurgeon could afford to take himself lightly—and also not take petty criticism so seriously. When someone reprimanded him for slipping humorous remarks into his sermons, he afterward remarked, "He would not blame me if he only knew how many of them I keep back."

Grace propelled this artist of the spirit. It enabled him to keep creating in his later years in spite of the debilitating pain brought on my rheumatic gout, and in spite of the severe depression that followed. It enabled him, above all, to honor. The one closest to him knew that best. Susannah Spurgeon, like her husband, suffered from serious illness. She remained a semi-invalid most of her life. But Charles never let her feel like a burden. Most driven men maintain only a token presence with their families, but everyone in the Spurgeon household knew they were cherished. When the Prince of Preachers died, one of those watching at his bedside with Susanna recalled her prayer: "We were touched beyond all expression . . . to hear the voice of the loved one, so sorely bereaved, thanking God for the many years that she had had the unspeakable joy of having such a precious husband lent to her."

Chapter Nine

BETTING ALL HIS RIGHTEOUSNESS

Charles Spurgeon's ventures in Victorian England show us a compelling alternative to traditional honor: honor as a verb, the extension of God's grace. Instead of falling back into the time-honored rut of carving out a respectable niche for ourselves, we concentrate on carving out a place for other people. Honor becomes something we give away rather than defend as a possession.

Spurgeon's gracious regard of England's most unpromising citizens grew directly out of the way God regarded him, the very particular regard called justification. God honored Spurgeon the sinner in a life-changing manner, and so he honored other people in the same way.

His evangelical emphasis on justification by faith is something many Adventists have rediscovered in recent decades. Many have come to see that all our doctrines must relate to this essential doctrine. We now remind each other that, after all, the three angels' messages are all given in the context of the "everlasting gospel." It is now proclaimed that Christ's ministry in the sanctuary really highlights the way in which His sacrifice on the cross saves us, the way in which His perfect life substitutes for ours in the judgment.

Even the seventh-day Sabbath is portrayed, in Hebrews, as a symbol of our rest in Christ's finished work.

The gospel has been making a comeback and slowly overcoming old, legalistic ways of thinking in the church. It's given us a better picture of God. Now we need to take a step further. We need it to give us a bigger picture of our religion; we need it to enlarge the way we live.

Attaining right standing with God in the courts of heaven may not seem like a burning, everyday issue. But in fact this matter of the atonement is the key that turns honor inside out. It is revolutionary in more than just a theological sense.

The Tragic Flaw

To begin to understand what a profound difference God's special regard can make in human life, we need to go back a ways to one of the influential myths that has shaped man's view of himself. The story of Achilles, from Greek mythology, still echoes in our world today.

According to legend, Achilles's mother, wanting to bestow immortality on her son, took him to the Styx River and plunged him in its waters. As a result his entire body became invulnerable to mortal blows—except for one spot: the heel by which she had held him in the water.

Achilles grew up to become a great hero. The ancient poets recounted a series of noble exploits involving the siege of Troy. Achilles defended Iphigenia, a young princess condemned to die as a sacrifice. When the Greeks had to retreat, he saved the day; rival Trojans trembled before his mighty sword. Later he pushed them back to the very gates of Troy, his armor glowing like fire.

The version of this tale that has most endured in people's minds describes Achilles falling in love with a daughter of Priam and coming unarmed to the temple of Apollo to be married to the princess. But there the treacherous Paris gave him a mortal wound in that one vulnerable spot—his heel. [1]

And so the Greeks gave us an enduring image: Achilles heel, the tragic flaw. The great hero who involves himself in many noble exploits is tragically defeated by that one thing that makes him vulnerable. The exposed heel became a symbol for a character blemish, something like pride, for example, which proved to be the downfall of more than one Greek hero.

The idea of the tragic flaw is still part of the self-portrait many people cling to. It's a perennial theme in literary tragedies and, on a smaller scale, in everyday life. Man the noble creature is defeated by some unfortunate flaw. If it just weren't for that little problem with booze or that occasional outburst at home, everything would be fine. We often look at our lives through this myth of the hero betrayed by a tragic element in the plot. The myth has been absorbed as part of humanism which proclaims that man is essentially good, evolving toward an ever-higher destiny, but still tripped up by certain flaws.

A Flash of Faith

Scripture presents us with a very different way of understanding ourselves. Its history of the plan of redemption turns the tragic flaw on its head. When Jehovah decided to form a special nation to preserve His truths in the ancient world, he did not select as first citizen some Achilles with blazing armor, massive spear, and resume of noble exploits. He chose a man who was simply willing to be nudged into an open-ended odyssey. Abram followed God's call, not knowing where his final destination lay.

During his time of settling in Canaan, Abram had good days and bad days. He could be generous with nephew Lot and empathetic toward wicked Sodom. He could also lie repeatedly to the authorities about his wife in order to protect his own neck. He could be a gracious host to strangers and yet act cruelly toward Hagar, the woman he took as concubine.

When making offerings to God on those stone altars, Abram could lift up only a very mixed bag of achievements. God might have easily focused on flaws. His habit of lying to get out of a tight spot, for example, could have become the central theme of the story, his Achilles heel leading to a tragic downfall. But God intervened and maneuvered Abram around the potential tragedies. That's not the way he wanted the story to end.

God chose to focus on a single, promising quality. One night Abram couldn't sleep. He lay there fretting about God's promise to make of him a great nation. The man was getting old; his wife Sarah had long passed childbearing age, and they still had no heir. How could the promise be fulfilled now? Abram whispered a complaint heavenward: "You have given me no children."

God's reply was to invite him out of his tent and under the stars. Gazing up at the vast, speckled sky, Abram heard God promise, "So shall your offspring be." [2]

God was trying to tap into a certain trait, reaching for the quality that had moved this man out of the comforts of Mesopotamia and into a divine adventure. And God found it. Abraham responded; he believed that his Lord would do the impossible.

Then God responded too. He looked down at this aging nomad under the stars, stretching on the tiptoes of his faith, and he saw an Achilles covered in resplendent armor. God counted Abram's faith as moral heroism, as righteousness. He chose not to look at the flaws, but to focus entirely on this one flash of faith in the dark.

And so Abram would become Abraham, the man in covenant with God, the father of faith. He would still stumble sometimes; his flaws would tumble out; he would make serious mistakes. But God kept regarding him as His chosen one, the one who'd accepted His wonderful promise in faith.

God kept working on that one redeemable quality, instead of zeroing in on the tragic flaws. And in the end it did become heroic. The faith that God had awakened and nurtured bore fruit. Standing one day on Mount Moriah, Abraham lifted up a knife in his trembling hand above his only son Isaac, bound on an altar of sacrifice. He stretched faith to its outer limits, clinging in terror to the hope that God would supply the sacrifice. Abraham, the man destined to communicate the faith to a whole nation, felt for a few moments something of what God the Father would feel looking down on the sacrifice of His Son. This patriarch experienced the passion at the heart of the covenant.

God's Narrowed Gaze

Throughout Scripture people encounter a God who wants to redeem them, who works to find a way to regard them as righteous. Tragic flaws are not the theme. We don't find noble creatures moved through a series of heroic deeds and then defeated by some kink in their characters. We find ordinary people moved to greatness because God regards them through some gesture of faith, some moment of stretching out.

All these adventures are summed up in Paul's great exposition:

God justifies the ungodly. He champions this good news most clearly in his epistle to the Romans. Chapters one and two present an insurmountable problem: humanity's habitual cruelty is acted out in front of a Creator who is uncompromisingly just. How are people ever going to find the union with Him necessary for ultimate survival if their deeds constantly disrespect His holiness? No matter how uprightly secular or ceremoniously religious we try to be, our integrity just never adds up to what the law requires. We fall silent looking at the wide gap between what we know to be right and what we do.

Having outlined the apparent checkmate our moral failures place us in, Paul introduces God's winning move in chapter three. It is God's leap of faith (not ours). He promises to justify us on the basis of faith in Christ Jesus alone, apart from our moral performance. He is willing to bet everything on that one gesture, that one glimmer of redeemability.

He can do so only because of Christ's performance that climaxed on the cross. In the definitive act of honoring, Jesus became man's legal substitute. He stood in our place as the condemned, unyielding before the taunts of enemies and the betrayal of friends, steady beneath the crushing weight of the Father's abandonment. And so those who accept this honor of the shed blood are counted as forgiven. In that blood Jesus spilled His righteous life out for us, the perfect sum of His obedience in the flesh. And so He can stand in our place before God as the righteous one. All those who accept this honor of Christ's white robe covering them are "accepted in the Beloved."

In chapter four, Paul builds on the case of Abraham who looked up at the stars that night and accepted God's promise of countless descendants. Paul explains that God chooses to honor our faith as His righteousness. In that one gesture He sees the whole. Reaching out to touch the passion of Christ we are enveloped in it and counted as part of it.

This is the perspective that rescues us. God narrows His gaze and looks only at our faith, not at our countless errors and chronic mistakes. He focuses with holy intensity on some gesture rather than the vast sickness within. Faith is only a gesture, but it becomes a handle God uses in snatching us out of our fate.

In chapter five, Paul seals his argument and makes explicit God's remarkable act of honor. The "abundant provision of grace" and the "gift of righteousness" flow to the unworthy through the "one man, Jesus Christ." Yes, "through the obedience of the one man the many will be made righteous."

This righteousness, this right standing with God, comes to us as a gift. It's grace, unmerited favor, unconditional acceptance—these definitions remind us that we have done nothing to deserve our privileged place. But it's also important to remember that God DOES seek something to value as He counts us righteous. Justification is not God saying: "You're a complete jerk but I'm going to pretend you're wonderful." That kind of regard is just a highly refined put down, a formal generosity which makes the unworthy feel all the more painfully indebted. Justification is God declaring: "You've joined yourself to My Son; I regard you as I regard Him. I'm going to treat you as what you can become."

Value Vs. Merit

Our redemption is a legal transaction, it does involve the payment of a debt, but it also involves the passion of the Father and Christ on the cross. They were not playing pretend on Golgotha. They were driven to sacrifice all for us by an immeasurably intense devotion. They are looking for something of value, something redeemable in everyone, even in those who pounded the nails into Christ's limbs. And so They are willing to regard even the most unpromising applicant for grace as a full-fledged member of the fraternity of the saved.

We have value, but we don't have merit. A great many Christians down through the centuries have tripped over that fine distinction and tumbled into theological warfare. Some want to emphasize God's sovereign act of grace and so define human beings as depraved wretches who possesses not a speck of worth in their whole sin-saturated beings. Others want to emphasize human cooperation with God's act of grace and declare that people can attain merit and make themselves worthy, or worthier, of that grace.

Both points of view chafe against the whole truth. We have value. However far we may have strayed, we bear the imprint of God's image within us. No human being is worthless. When we reach out in faith to Christ, that is something of value; it is precious; it is promising; it is a piece of the whole. Faith is not a zero.

But faith is not merit. It doesn't earn anything. We may have something of value but that still doesn't measure up to the glory of God, to

His character. Faith is not a down payment on a costly salvation to be followed by regular payments of good works for the rest of our lives. Making a promising gesture and measuring up to God's standards are completely separate things. The former is something within us that God graciously focuses on; the later is something that Jesus Christ accomplishes—totally apart from us.

All this relates back to dark humility: trying to squash man into the mud in order to exalt God. We don't need to build this caricature of wretched-worm humanity in order to demonstrate that we fall short of God's requirements. He is far above our best efforts. We consistently come up short even of our own mediocre moral expectations.

It is God's act of honoring alone which overshadows our tragic flaws. He still hopes. He's still willing to bet all his righteousness on us. He's still able to count as whole those who make that first gesture of faith.

Justification can appear to be the most esoteric of Christian doctrines, an elaborate legal fiction perpetrated to please some unfathomable divine necessity. But it really lies at the center of God's self-revelation. It spotlights something fundamental in God's character: His gracious regard. And that can transform human life.

It's often said that all doctrines revolve around the Cross. Our moral life revolves around the atonement as well. God's honoring is the fountain from which all our relationships must take their inspiration. It splashes color on that little word love which we've tried to make carry so much ethical weight.

All the richness of God's character is involved in His honoring, the source spills over to its object. This is what we must express. This is how we come to hard honor. It's based on two beams of wood impaling the earth, firm, unshakable. God regards us graciously, though we mock Him, beat Him, and gamble for His garments as He suffers in hell.

Hard honor doesn't go with the flow or depend on the trend. It doesn't look for tragic flaws or reasons to exclude. It counts every human being as redeemable. It constantly looks for some promising quality, some crack through which grace may find an entry.

The Cross turns "honor the possession" into "honor the gift." All the richness of traditional honor—its uniforms, codes, titles, coat-of-arms, privileges—all are uprooted and bestowed. The believer's honor is in honoring, in the hard honor of regarding others with the Redeemer's unchanging grace.

Chapter Ten

THE EPIC OF HARD HONOR

Scripture has its own tale of honor, a story which dramatizes honor the verb, honor given away, and shows us just how radically different our Redeemer's point of view really is.

We start with a dramatic conflict in the courts of King Saul. Here we find the biblical counterpart to all those knights in shining armor upholding their code of chivalry and battling for their honor. Two rivals met in the palace one day: Jonathan, the son of King Saul, and a rising military hero named David. One stood in line to the throne, the other had been anointed by the prophet Samuel to occupy it. There should have been jealousy and plotting and backstabbing between them. There should have been a struggle for "rightful honor." Instead a heroic friendship would blossom.

David had been invited to the palace after he killed the Philistine champion Goliath. But Saul began to hate this poet-warrior after his exploits threatened to overshadow his own. One day, he hurled a spear at David as he played his harp and the young man had to flee into hiding.

Prince Jonathan faced a dilemma. He was bound by blood and royal tradition to his father. And his whole future was on the line—on

Saul's side. And yet he had already found in David a kindred spirit.

This was a time of moral slip-sliding-away in Israel. The Hebrews faced belligerent Philistine armies. For them, the God of Abraham, Isaac, and Jacob had shrunk. He could be threatened. Their leader had abandoned prophetic guidance.

A Knight's Emblems

But David and Jonathan had somehow escaped the erosion of belief all around them; they clung to the same spunky faith. When David had brought bread and roasted grain to his soldier brothers in the Valley of Elah and peeked over the ravine toward the enemy troops, he didn't think of how well-armed they were. He wondered at the inactivity of the "armies of the living God." When Goliath, the Philistine robo-warrior, stepped out (as he'd done for fourty mornings) and issued his make-my-day challenge, David didn't tremble with the others; he was appalled that this man should defy the God of heaven. This shepherd lad went out to meet the giant and leveled him "in the name of the Lord Almighty."

Not long before this, Jonathan had his own solo adventure against the Philistines in a mountain pass at Micmash. He talked his armor-bearer into sneaking up with him to the enemy camp in a crevasse between two cliffs. Jonathan believed that "Nothing can hinder the Lord from saving, whether by many or by few," and so he ventured out to test that proposition.

Jonathan asked the Lord for a sign. He would show himself to the men in the outpost; if they said "Come up to us," this would indicate God approved the mission. Never mind how outnumbered the two might be, or how suicidal the mission appeared on "parchment," the only thing that mattered was whether the Living God was with them.

Jonathan and armor-bearer popped out behind a rock, waved at the Philistines and received the requested invitation: "Come on up so we can bash your heads in." Hearing this, Jonathan urged his friend, "Climb up after me; the Lord has given them into the hand of Israel," as if the outcome had already been decided. As it turned out, the two Hebrews killed about twenty men and sent the rest of the Philistine army into a panic. [1]

Imagine what it was like for David and Jonathan to meet in that palace, each one an isolated oasis of courageous faith in a vast desert of stunted belief—to finally find the same fire in the eyes of another after nurturing it alone so long. No wonder their souls were knit together.

Jonathan's commitment to David as the rightful successor grew, but so did his father's rage. Saul wanted David dead and tried to pressure Jonathan into cooperating. At dinner one day, he tried to pound some sense into the youth: "You idiot, don't you know that as long as you side with David you will never be established as king." Jonathan wanted to know what wrong David had done to deserve death. Exasperated, Saul grabbed a spear and hurled it at his son. Jonathan left the table unscathed, but broken with shame at what his father had become.

He secretly met with his soul mate and managed to keep him out of harm's way. At the same time, he would not completely deny his father. He went with him into his final doomed battle on Mount Gilboa, where both were killed.

There is one moment in the extraordinary friendship of Jonathan and David that speaks of the whole. In that time and place of disintegrating relationships, Jonathan wanted to express his loyalty through a covenant. This prince took off his royal robe and placed it around David's shoulders. He gave him his tunic and belt, his sword and bow. Jonathan was, in effect, crowning the future king, the man who would take his place in history. And he did it with enthusiastic devotion. To find someone whose soul burned with the same faith—this meant everything. He would honor that above everything else, even his own future.

Here we have the knight in shining armor, the prince distinguished by heroic deeds, bestowing the emblems of his honor on another. The royal robe, the gleaming sword that had vanquished the enemy, were not possessions to defend, but means to honor a friend. The Bible turns the knight of chivalry upside down. Honor gallops out of the castle and becomes a verb. The armor we've kept polished for centuries as our honorable emblem is turned into clothing for the needy.

Revenge of a Different Cloth

A little later in the narrative we find a story that takes on the theme of revenge, traditional honor's oldest and most trusted companion. All those indignant duelists pacing off in opposite directions should stop a moment and look at a certain Hebrew fugitive.

David spent many months running about the desert of En Gedi trying to keep at least one rocky hill between himself and King Saul. He had plenty to avenge. He, the rightful heir to the throne, had to live like a fugitive. His persecutor had forfeited his kingship by disobeying Samuel, but still cling fiercely to power.

One day, David got his golden opportunity. Saul had marched into En Gedi with three thousand choice soldiers selected from all Israel. This time he wasn't going to let wily David get away. While his men rested near the Crag of the Wild Goats, Saul went into a cave to relieve himself—the very cave where David and his band were hiding. There he was, this usurper, alone and pathetically vulnerable. David's men urged him to get satisfaction and avenge his slandered name. Surely this was God fulfilling his promise to "give your enemies into your hands."

David crept forward in the dark and drew his knife. But he couldn't bring himself to harm Saul. Instead he cut off a corner of the king's robe and crawled back to his men. They were flabbergasted, no doubt whispering fiercely, "Why didn't you kill him for God's sake?"

But David replied, "The Lord forbid that I should do such a thing to my master, the Lord's anointed." He had to restrain his men from going after Saul themselves. The king walked out untouched.

David had seen something besides his persecutor there in the cave, something besides a man perversely obsessed. He saw a person whom God had once anointed, just as he himself had been anointed. He saw a king who early in his reign had rescued the city of Jabesh and led Israel heroically accompanied by "valiant men whose hearts God had touched."

David even felt remorse for laying a hand on Saul's royal robe, perhaps remembering the princely garment that had so graciously been placed on his shoulders. This fugitive had to honor the one whom God had once chosen. He would not lift his hand against him, surely somewhere there must be something redeemable left in the man.

David walked out of the cave with his men and called out "My Lord the king!" He prostrated himself before Saul and then made his appeal, lifting up the piece of royal cloth that Saul now realized, white-faced, was missing: "See, my father . . . I have not wronged you." [2]

David's eloquent act of honor had its effect. He did strike something redeemable. Saul broke down and wept: "You are more righteous than I. You have treated me well, but I have treated you badly." He acknowledged David's right to rule Israel, summoned his three thousand crack troops and went home.

Later Saul's demons would overwhelm that moment of redemption and he began pursuing David again, not really stopping until he met his end on Mount Gilgal. But David's act of honor still shines out as artful goodness at its best. He reverses the long and proud tradition of revenge. Instead of wresting satisfaction from his stubborn foe, David honored him as the anointed. He saw him through his original calling.

For a time this young king-to-be stopped in its tracks the endless convulsion of assassination and counter-assassination that so often moved people to and through the throne. His act of honoring raised up a wall against it. Toward the end of Israel's history we see the terrible spectacle of people killing to be king. How invaluable David's act of honoring must have been during the Golden Age before Israel's long, tragic decline.

Bestowing Purity

Scripture also takes on the honor of the pure maiden in her ivory tower who defends her untouched status like prime real estate—chastity used as a coat of arms, a status symbol. We get the Bible's perspective in the classic romance story of Ruth and Boaz.

A wealthy landowner of Bethlehem, Boaz, was out checking on the barley harvest one day when he spotted a young woman working the edges of his field. He watched her labor all day, picking up stalks the harvesters had left behind. Boaz asked about the girl and heard the remarkable story of Ruth, a widow from Moab who had left her country to come and care for her aging mother-in-law Naomi.

During a break one afternoon, Boaz approached the girl. As an impoverished foreigner working alone, Ruth was vulnerable out in the fields. So Boaz extended his protection: "My daughter . . . don't go and glean in another field. Stay here with my servant girls. I have told the men not to touch you. And whenever you are thirsty, go and get a drink from the water jars the men have filled." [3]

Surprised by this act of kindness, Ruth asked, "Why have I found such favor in your eyes that you notice me—a foreigner?"

Boaz told her that he admired her faithfulness to Naomi and her courage in coming to this new land. He said, "May you be richly rewarded by the Lord, the God of Israel, under whose wings you have come to take refuge."

Boaz was a powerful man in his community. It would have been easy for him to take advantage of this attractive widow. But he treated Ruth with courtesy and respect. He didn't see some unclean alien, or a servant girl beneath his class, but a woman with a beautiful character.

As the harvest progressed, Boaz continued to show kindness to Ruth. He instructed his men, "Even if she gathers among the sheaves, don't embarrass her. Rather, pull out some stalks for her from the bundles and leave them for her to pick up, and don't rebuke her."

Naomi began hearing about the man's attentions to her daughter-in-law and realized he was a relative, a kinsman-redeemer, one who could marry the widow of a deceased relative in order to produce children who could carry on the relative's name. Naomi saw that Boaz was attracted to Ruth, and Ruth spoke warmly of him. It was the custom for the widow to make the formal proposal to the kinsman-redeemer, so one day Naomi carefully instructed Ruth in how to present herself to Boaz.

That evening Boaz was alone, threshing barley near his fields. A steady breeze blew in from the Mediterranean during the hours before sunset. After the chaff had been blown away and the day's harvest lay in a neat pile of grain, Boaz lay down to sleep. He would be there all night, guarding the barley.

As Boaz slept, Ruth approached quietly in the dark. She lifted his blanket and lay down at his feet. This was a symbolic gesture. Among the Hebrews, marriages were solemnized by the man throwing his robe over the woman.

Boaz woke up and peered into the dark. "Who are you?" he whispered.

"I am your servant, Ruth," came the reply. "Spread the corner of your garment over me, since you are my kinsman-redeemer."

Boaz happily answered: "The Lord bless you, my daughter. This kindness is greater than that which you showed earlier . . .

And now . . . don't be afraid. I will do for you all you ask."

Ruth had literally thrown herself at his feet, but Boaz didn't gloat over his conquest. He spoke of a kindness SHE had shown, and thanked her as a "woman of noble character." Knowing that people might get the wrong idea about her visit, he kept the circumstances a secret.

This story has many of the ingredients found in tales of a gallant knight winning a beautiful virgin. But all of Boaz's protective courtesies were directed at a widow, not some virgin enshrined in a lofty tower. He honored an impoverished gleaner who was burned by the sun and smudged by the soil. He treated the girl with all the delicate consideration one would give the fairest, most innocent maiden. The important thing for him was not moving into prime real estate no one else had touched, but honoring Ruth and respecting her good qualities.

The traditional emphasis of sexual honor was in defending turf, carefully regulating property values, as it were, so that a supply of untouched women could be preserved for knights who wanted to settle down. But biblical honor BESTOWS purity. To a certain extent, purity is something we can give. In the eye of the beholder, it helps create and nurture that very quality in the lovingly.

The World Re-titled

In the book of Acts, we find a story that challenges all those titles that were so essential in the old world of honor: the elite in resplendent uniforms, the elaborate deferences, the choice banquet positions. The Bible, in effect, re-titles the world. A man named Ananias leads the way.

He was waiting in Damascus for the coming of a persecutor who had killed many Christians. Everyone had heard of the brilliant young Saul of Tarsus who'd carried out a campaign of harassment against believers in Jerusalem. This man had been given authority by the Sanhedrin to take into custody any followers of Jesus he might find in Damascus.

Ananias and the other believers surely prayed earnestly that somehow this grand inquisitor might be stopped. And he was. News spread through the city that the Saul had stumbled into town completely blind, a soldier leading him by the hand. Instead of ferreting out Christians, he was holed up in the house of Judas on Straight Street. Ananias was of course overjoyed. The enemy had been struck down. That was the good news.

But then Ananias had a vision. God instructed him to go to that very house of Judas on Straight Street, lay his hands on Saul of Tarsus, and restore his sight. This command seemed incomprehensible. Ananias reminded his Lord that Saul had come to town "to arrest all who call on your name." But the voice told him to go anyway, and informed him that Saul was now "my chosen instrument" who would spread the word to the Gentiles.

Impossible! Saul the Pharisee of Pharisees now Jesus' evangelist? Most of us would have demanded proof, or at least a probationary period. After all, there was so much to forgive. This man had the blood of saints on his hands.

But Ananias chose the perspective of faith. He focused on God's statement that Saul was a chosen instrument. Walking over to Straight Street, he knocked on the door of Judas (yes, the name that shouted of betrayal) and was ushered in. Just like that he placed his hands on the blind man there and said, "Brother Saul . . ."[4]

I'm impressed by the fact that Ananias prayed and Saul was healed. I am impressed by that fact that he prayed for the Holy Spirit to fall on Saul and baptized him. I am impressed by the fact that Ananias and other believers spent several days teaching Saul all they knew about Christ. But I am most moved by those first two words Ananias uttered. He called the grand inquisitor "Brother Saul" just on the strength of God's honoring the man as a chosen instrument.

In that word of welcome I see all the titles and trappings and uniforms of the world absorbed. "Brother" becomes a name that supersedes all others. It was a title that Ananias courageously gave away. Christ has laid down his life. The world is turned upside down and inside out with redeemability. We can become children of God forever and say the word "Brother" as a welcome into fellowship with Him. The world is re-titled.

Precise Honor

In the narratives of Christ's life we find examples of an honor honed to surgical precision. Out of the whole populace of Capernaum shoving and clawing its way close to the miracle-worker, Jesus felt that one timid, desperate touch from the woman who'd been hemorrhaging for twelve years. He stopped the town in its tracks and singled her out: "Daughter, take courage; your faith has made you well."

When the disciples tried to move some runny-nosed kids out of the way for more important visitors, Jesus honored the undervalued, not with some condescending pablum about how sweet they looked, but by pointing out their guileless faith. It was a quality their elders needed to imitate: "Unless you become like this little child. . . ."

Jesus' contemporaries argued endlessly about who might qualify as a person's neighbor. There was no question that the Gentiles were not, so no obligations toward them existed. But what about a person who was ceremonially unclean? What about those of the Samaritan sect?

Here was traditional honor at work. How can the elite behave in a way that maintains their position? But Jesus turned the question of "Who is my neighbor?" on its head. He told a story that emphasized how to be a good neighbor. The Good Samaritan honored someone who would have walked on by had the tables been turned. The issue was not how may I maintain my honor, but how may I honor.

In His discourses, Jesus leaped above the law to artful goodness. It's not enough to avoid murder. We must work to avoid writing people off as fools, as unredeemable. We cannot judge another; a critic is not looking for that window of redeemability; he's looking for Achilles's heel. Jesus pushed honor to specific extremes: if someone slaps you on the cheek, turn to him the other one. If you have a sworn enemy, pray for him. In any and every situation, we must honor our neighbor.

Here we have a different knight indeed, one whose battle is to defend not just those fair maidens in ivory towers but also those stuck in the mud at the bottom of the moat.

Reaching for the Redeemable

As he matured in his faith, the apostle Paul became embedded in the hard honor of the atonement. He grew into a champion of God's will to mercy, that immovable rock of grace that refused to budge on Golgotha when humanity pressed its ugliest face against it. Paul consistently honored all the imperfect, troublesome individuals under his care.

I see Paul's honor best amid the deafening roar of a mob in Jerusalem. He'd been seen near the temple with a Greek friend and people assumed he'd brought the man inside and "defiled this holy place." Some Jews from the province of Asia began shouting that Paul was going all over the world slandering everything they held sacred. Word spread through the streets and people came running.

They dragged Paul out of the temple, quickly shut its gates (as if to keep it from further pollution), and began pounding on the man viciously. Fortunately, the Roman commander in Jerusalem heard about the commotion and hurried to the site with his soldiers. Seeing him coming, the rioters stepped back from the man they were about to beat to death.

The commander quickly arrested this troublemaker lying in his blood and bound him with two chains. He then asked the mob what crime he'd committed. They began yelling out accusations with such ferocity that the commander thought they'd better take Paul into the barracks. The soldiers barely managed to shove their way through the mob, which kept flailing at Paul.

Finally they reached the steps of the barracks and relative safety. But before they could go in, Paul revived himself enough to make a request. He wanted to speak to the crowd. The commander must have done a double take. Paul had barely escaped a brutal death; he was just about to be rescued, but now he wanted to turn toward the contorted faces screaming for his blood and have a few words.

For some reason the commander gave his permission. Paul stood up on the steps, motioned to the crowd, and, when they quieted a bit, said, "brothers and sisters, listen now to my defense." The crowd fell silent. Paul proceeded to tell the story of his conversion, and through it make an appeal to his countrymen.

Brothers. Paul was now sharing the title that had once been given to him so graciously. The bruised and bloodied apostle saw more than the faces of rage out there. He saw people who could be redeemed. This was no abstract humanity in the distance, easy to honor in theory. These were raging fanatics, up close and personal. But hard honor would not let him retreat from that spectacle. Paul reached for the redeemable human being behind the frenzied caricature. And for a few moments, at least, he touched the mob.

Chapter Eleven

PERFUME POURED OUT BEFOREHAND

Patriarch, prince, and prophet set before us the epic tale of hard honor, one of those values which turns the world upside down. And that story too points us toward the New Testament epistles where the quality is given explicit authority. "Outdo one another in showing honor," [1] says Paul. Peter commands: "Honor all men. Love the brotherhood." [2] Husbands are to be considerate, "bestowing honor on the woman, as the weaker sex, since you are joint heirs of the grace of life." [3]

In Ephesians, Paul declares that men are to regard their wives as if they were Christ looking on His church, giving Himself up for her. Wives in turn are to see Christ in their husbands and affirm that potential. Both sexes are to submit to one another out of reverence for Christ. [4]

Paul continues: "Children honor your father and mother, parents honor your children by disciplining them without anger, as those entrusted to you by the Lord. Servants do your work as if for the Lord. Masters give up threatening, be impartial, regard slaves not as slaves but as brothers in Christ." [5]

Honor is the first and last word in the way we relate to other people. Listen to Peter: "To sum up, let all be harmonious, sympathetic, brotherly, kindhearted, and humble in spirit; not returning evil for evil, or insult for insult, but giving a blessing instead;" [6]

New Testament teaching gives this hard honor a functional shape. It suggests the components it's made of and what it accomplishes.

Through the Clutter

John defines love as God sending "his Son as an atoning sacrifice for our sins." [7] His blood covers a world full of terrible wrongdoing. Hard honor begins from this point; it is the love that covers a multitude of sins, it sweeps away the garbage.

This quality is immensely useful first of all as a clearing agent. It eliminates all kinds of conditions and expectations that people huffing and puffing indignantly erect as barriers. Just as light humility gets us past all the useless baggage that an insecure ego can pile up inside us, so hard honor gets us past all the pettiness that can interfere with our relationships with others.

Just inside the vestibule, we peered cautiously at the long pews and smattering of saints, not at all sure that our faded jeans and unkempt hair would find a welcome. After all, this was 1972 and we college students looked far too much like "filthy, flag-burnin' hippies" to the good folk of Tulsa, Oklahoma. But we were stuck there, and the little Baptist chapel seemed to be our only alternative.

Soon an elderly lady came over and invited us to sit down for "Reverend Johnson's talk." We scooted into a pew at the back of the small church and listened to the pastor deliver his Sunday vespers message with simple, unadorned conviction. Behind him, on the bare white wall hung a tiny picture of Jesus.

After smiling our way through greetings at the end of the service, we explained our problem. On the way back from a summer Christian training conference in Dallas, our bus had broken down and was towed to a filling station nearby. Most of the kids had taken a Greyhound home; five of us had decided to stay and try to get the bus fixed. Unfortunately we'd discovered that the mechanics at the gas station were dishonest.

The church folk were eager to help, especially a Mr. John Reed who had a mechanic friend. "Why we'll have 'er runnin' in no time," he said cheerfully. "Ralph can fix most anything."

After a phone call, Ralph the mechanic came by and opened up the hood. Ron, the other driver, and I tried in vain to recall meaningful symptoms for him: "Well we were driving along the highway and . . . it quit . . . just died."

Ralph climbed into our venerable yellow school bus and turned the key. The engine responded with a token groan. After he poked around under the bus for a while it became clear that our vehicle wouldn't be fixed that night. But Mr. Reed—slightly balding, open-faced and freckled—had an idea: "Listen, you all can come over and stay at our house. We've got plenty of room. We'll get this thing goin' in the morning."

The five of us couldn't come up with any of the polite refusals that usually keep strangers from barging in. There was just our suddenly retired bus and the empty night. So we gratefully climbed into Mr. Reed's 1961 station wagon.

We made our way to a modest suburban home in a blue-collar neighborhood, and John and Evelyn Reed made room. The house had seen a lot of living and showed no traces of luxury, but in some mysterious way Mr. Green and his wife made the thought that we were imposing slip from our minds. It was like we were their kids home from college. A sofa here, a few cots on the screened porch there, and everyone was settled.

It took a good part of the next day to find engine parts. John drove us around, pointing out the "sights" of Tulsa. Other men from the church came in the evening. They joked together, drank Evelyn's coffee, and installed the parts, while we collegiates stood around faking assistance. Finally, our bus started in earnest. The men cheered, had a final cup, and departed in the night.

Tuesday morning, after a savory meal of biscuits, scrambled eggs and grits, we boarded our purring vehicle and thanked the Reeds profusely. We had nothing but thanks; they had provided everything else. As Chris, the lone girl in our group, cried half-cheerfully, we waved from the windows and pulled out.

After a couple of miles through the suburbs, our bus began to screech. The clatter reverberated from different places, cleverly disguising the source of the problem. Ron and I jumped out and opened the hood. We stared at the engine for what seemed a respectfully long enough time, poking around, commenting sagely to each other—"Yeah, that's the radiator all right."

Pulling up noisily at the now familiar blue frame house, we smiled sheepishly at John Reed and explained, "It started making awful noises."

This time it took two days to fix. But the Reeds remained gracious: "Great, you kids can come to prayer meeting with us."

At the little Baptist chapel a warbling organ cranked out hymns that I had always thought rather dull. But that night, singing among those square jaws and weathered faces, I caught a new warmth from the old familiar phrases.

Pastor Johnson asked if we would get up and "testify" about the Lord's blessing at our conference. The five of us went up to the creaky wooden platform one by one and talked about what we'd learned. John and Evelyn beamed at us, looking like proud parents at a graduation.

Afterwards, everyone enthusiastically thanked us. We had said little, but they called it a "wonderful blessing." Our Okie friends felt like their small isolated congregation was now bound to the larger body of Christ.

Thursday morning brought another tearful farewell. Our bus lumbered along amiable for an entire two blocks before falling fast asleep in third gear. It couldn't be coaxed awake. A highway patrolman dropped by. We tried to explain that friends just down the road could help us in just a few minutes, but he insisted that our bus had to be towed off the narrow road immediately. He radioed a truck and we were hauled across town to Ace Garage. I got on the phone: "John, it's me again."

"Well, I'll be. How far did you all get this time?" John wasn't upset. His voice sounded as affable as ever. "You sit tight, hear? We'll be over in a jiffy."

The five of us feasted on mashed potatoes, green beans and corn-on-the-cob. In the afternoon, Chris looked at old photo albums with Evelyn and the rest of us touched up the front siding and helped the Reed's twelve-year-old boy feed his rabbits. It felt good to be just family.

Friday morning. "This is going to be it," I said confidently. We waved to "mom" and "papa" Reed again through the bus windows and they stood for along time on their narrow crabgrass lawn.

At the outskirts of Tulsa, our crotchety yellow vehicle started hinting—little groans here and there. All was not well. The motor misfired; the hinting grew more persistent. Ron and I grimaced at each other and finally decided to turn around; there was no way we'd make it back to Illinois.

What would the Reeds say this time? Surely they wouldn't believe it; surely we'd catch a hint of tension in their faces. But no, Papa was out on the lawn waving as soon as our telltale sputtering could be heard coming up the street.

We apologized lamely, but John wouldn't hear of it: "Glad to have you back."

During our entire stay in Tulsa, we never saw a trace of the wearying strain that must come from having five extra people camp out in your home. The Reeds always managed to make us feel like we were honoring them, not they us. Tested to the limit, their welcome never flinched.

One guy in our group was African-American. The neighbors could not conceal their distress about his sleeping in their midst. But John told me quietly he was proud to be sheltering the young man.

We had popped out of the alien world of protesting, drug-invested universities into their Okie land of country music and the flag. Yet our two mutually intangible cultures presented no barriers. Mom and Papa Reed always treated us a blessing. They valued us for our fellowship, and accepted us, extra toothbrushes, sleeping bags, dirty socks, and all.

Sabbath arrived, our fourth attempt at departure. We embraced our adopted family and said hopeful, sad goodbyes. This time Chris's tears were not shed in vain.

Poured Full

The following Christmas my family took a trip south to Texas. We were passing by Tulsa on a Sunday when I suddenly remembered the little church close by the freeway and talked my parents into stopping for a few minutes.

When I stepped inside the chapel, the worship service was almost over. Pastor Johnson was preaching with the same conviction. After the last hymn, I picked out the Reeds among the parishioners under a high noon sun. I couldn't believe how thrilled they were that I'd come. Their happiness just rushed over me. Papa Reed kept telling my dumbfounded parents what a tremendous blessing we students had been to their church.

Those people's delight just because I was present struck at something deep inside. John's youngest, a seven-year-old, had been away at summer camp during the broken-down-bus episode. The girl had never laid eyes on me, but she ran over anyway and hugged my waist earnestly as if for a long-lost brother. At that moment, I felt I was poured into being.

As a kid in his late teens, I was still carving out a niche for myself. I had the usual struggles to fit in, to be cool. Would my zits ever go away? Was I wearing the right clothes? Were the lines I threw at pretty girls clever or moronic?

But in the warmth of that moment all those concerns were brushed aside. All the things I subconsciously used to make me feel valuable seemed insignificant. I had nothing with which to recommend myself. I became empty, illuminatingly so, and in that sudden vacuum experienced the grace of being poured full by their jubilation.

I suppose that church was no spiritual powerhouse. Sunday by Sunday, the believers gave their sincere but drowsy assent to the sermon. A casual visitor would probably catch little excitement from the group. But a potent honor simmered in that aged stone building squatting modestly by the rush of interstaters. That congregation disclosed to me "the grace of the Lord Jesus Christ," banners blowing. Their act of honor filled me to the brim.

Hard honor is tough enough to break through barriers. It creates a way to regard someone with grace even where there are no apparent grounds for it. When Jesus' act of honor is paramount, and His re-titling the world with the words "sister" and "brother" predominates, then all kinds of differences simply collapse.

As Adventists, we tend to erect a lot of barriers to "outsiders" even in our attempts to reach them. Sometimes we can't see past lifestyle differences to other values that we have in common. Sometimes doctrinal differences obscure the belief in Christ we share. And so we have a hard time acting graciously. We have a hard time honoring those who don't measure up.

But I will never forget the day I was poured into being by a group of people with whom I had nothing in common—except a Savior.

The apostle Paul took hard honor to its logical and revolutionary conclusion: "There is neither Jew nor Greek, slave nor free, male nor female, for you are all one in Christ Jesus." [8] Christ is all in all. His sacrifice trivializes all other human distinctions. Paul told the Corinthians that "the love of Christ controls us, because we are convinced that one has died for all." [9] Christ's death allows us to look on the world in a totally different way; He has placed a supreme value on each individual in it. "From now on, therefore," Paul continued, "we regard no one from a human point of view." The reconciliation is what determines perspective now. God is already reconciled to sinful human beings because of Christ's act of honor. Any alienation people may experience is strictly their doing, their choice.

Giving People Meaning

Hard honor drives through barriers. It also does something else. It gives people significance. God's act of honoring makes available a rich source of meaning. We can echo His creative regard. Hard honor can bestow unexpected significance even on the most aimless and dreary of lives.

Jesus and His disciples were reclining before a special festive supper six days before Passover in the home of Simon, a leper whom Jesus had healed. This was Bethany, the town of Christ's devoted followers Martha, Mary, and Lazarus. The town's inhabitants were making quite a big deal out of the Nazarene rabbi. They sensed His ministry might be heading toward a climax at Jerusalem. Word had spread among the crowds on pilgrimage to the Holy City that one of Jesus' followers had at one time been a corpse. Everyone wanted to see the man, Lazarus, and his healer. Christ's enemies had begun to circle for the kill. But their hands were temporarily tied by the admiring multitudes.

In this tense excitement, Simon hoped to honor the great Teacher and give Him a restful Friday evening. All was proceeding as planned, with Jesus and Lazarus reclining in honored places, when suddenly the guest room filled with a pungent fragrance. The nostrils of Judas were the first to identify and quantify it: pure nard, very expensive. He and the others who'd dropped their bread saw that Mary had crept in and was pouring an alabaster vial of the perfume on Jesus' head, as if anointing him. Then she moved down to remove his sandals. The woman rubbed his dust-streaked feet with the remainder of the nard and wiped them off with her hair.

Judas did some quick calculating. That was 300 days' wages evaporating into thin air. Noting the disturbed look on the faces around him, he declared that this perfume might have been sold for a good price and the proceeds placed in his fund—for the poor of course. Most of the disciples agreed; it did seem to be a costly gesture.

They were perhaps even more disturbed that a mere woman should be so forward. Was it really proper for her to be touching the spotless rabbi like this? What business did she have interrupting their pleasant evening? Several voices joined in Judas' criticism. Some reprimanded Mary directly. Her face flushed. She was about to beat a hasty retreat when Jesus silenced the guests with a sharp rebuke: "Leave her alone."

He knew that this woman's awkward act flowed out of a wealth of devotion. So He informed those frowning indignantly that this woman had done something beautiful. And then He immortalized her act by linking it to His coming passion. "She poured perfume on my body beforehand to prepare for my burial," He said. Jesus was about to place Himself in the hands of His enemies, endure a mock trial, suffer greatly on a cross, and lie cold and bloodless in a tomb. The climactic confrontation of His life was approaching. But His disciples couldn't grasp it; they offered no real companionship during this most difficult of journeys toward Jerusalem.

This woman at His feet, however, had touched Him in His hour of need. And Jesus honored that. He transformed her gesture of blind devotion into a companion piece, a part of the spectacle of the atonement. He said, in effect, "Only this woman, among you all, has echoed ultimate truth. Only she is identified with Me in the great ordeal ahead."

Jesus lifted up Mary's act as an emblem for all the redeemed down through the ages, all those who would come to honor His sacrifice with 20-20 hindsight as much as she honored it impulsively from the heart. Mary heard these words: "Wherever the gospel is preached throughout the world, what she has done will also be told, in memory of her."

Jesus honored the dishonored one by giving her meaning. It was His insight into the significance of her act that redeemed her from the shadows. Mary could take home that alabaster vial, now fittingly empty, and walk tall amid the gossips of Bethany. She'd become part of the Messiah's sacrifice; no one would ever take that away from her.

Creating Personhood

Hard honor carves meaning out of the rough stone. It is Michaelangelo seeing an angel in the shapeless mass of rock. By getting past exteriors and imparting significance, hard honor creates personhood. The apostle Paul's fruitful ministry was based on the premise that a believer stands before the righteous God "holy and blameless and beyond reproach." He liked to assure his listeners: "In Him you have been made complete." This apostle extended generous divine grace in all his own relationships. He labored with all his energy to "present every man complete in Christ." He believed that the wholeness which God saw by faith in every individual would seep into the innermost being.

People are much more fragile than we usually think, especially in that inner sanctum where self-worth struggles to bloom. Macho quarterbacks and beauty queens as well as pimpled nerds and business failures desperately need a sense of value that goes beyond accomplishments. It needs to be separate from what we do or don't do. Hard honor is what creates personhood.

I walked into room 307 with three clean sheets and a plastic bag, not knowing exactly what to expect. It was the first night I'd received Mr. Griffin's Patient Care Card. A nurse's aid told me he'd had a stroke. I hoped the man could at least roll over for his bed bath.

Griffin lay still on his back in the semi-private room. As he breathed very slowly, the sheet undulated over his large belly. I figured he weighed close to 180 pounds.

Griffin was my last patient. I wanted to get through with him fast so I could have some time to finish the last chapter of a book I'd been reading, *The Biblical Meaning of History*. It had been a long evening of hustling bedpans and drawsheets. Too many little red lights flashed above patient's doorways that shift. Too many incontinent bowels, gurgling throats, crabby cardiacs, and moody post-operatives. I was ready for the big recliner in the orderly lounge.

After quickly checking Griffin's pulse and temperature, I began tucking the sheets under him. As I moved to roll him over, he tried to speak. I leaned close. The patient lifted his eyebrows, nodded his head, twisted his lips, flayed with his tongue—but no words came out. A few syllables, however, and a pointing of his wide eyes got across the message.

"OK," I told him, "the john."

It was very hard hoisting his torso up into a sitting position. Griffin was dead weight. I popped out in the hall; the other orderlies are busy. Just my luck. Well, I'd rather get this over with fast anyway.

There was an aluminum walker in the room; maybe that would help. "Mr. Griffin can you use the walk . . . oh, never mind." I placed it beside the bed. I pulled his slightly mobile left arm over my shoulder, encircled his waist, and grunted and heaved the man upright.

Griffin leaned toward the walker, tottered on his stiff legs and collapsed in my arms. Make that 200 pounds. The back of his hospital gown flew open and his bare buttocks pressed against my thigh. Well, forget the stupid walker. Taking a deep breath, I locked my arms around his chest and dragged him roughly across the room to the bathroom door. His dry, flaking feet slid lifelessly over the green tiles.

My patient struggled to move his good arm, trying to be of assistance. But I just kept dragging. In the heat of my exertion, I silently cursed his bulk and nearly dropped the man while swinging his back around to the toilet. But we make it down all right. I shut the door and left him for a while.

Time for a break.

Only much later did I realize that I had acted dishonorably. Mr. Griffin had become for me a bag of meat, a task requiring the shortest distance between bed and toilet. I didn't sense that he was already distraught over his apparently healthy limbs that refused to budge on command. He did not need some impatient orderly to emphasize his helplessness. In my hurried round of "patient care" I forgot that those pale cheeks could flush with shame like any man's. The intelligence and pain reflected in his eyes escaped me. I was in too much of a hurry to get back and discover the true "Biblical Meaning of History."

That incident, however, led me into one of my first introductions to the meaning of honor.

Mr. Harvey existed in the geriatric ward, one of those patients who lay immobile in a no-man's land between the living and the dead. They told me he was only about fifty, but his pale skin stretched taut across a gaunt face. His mouth hung open, his breathing hardly perceptible. Once in a while his heart was moved to beat regularly.

Although at times his eyes moved, Harvey seemed unaware of his surroundings. His many ailments kept him shuttling between county and state hospitals. I'd overheard a doctor saying something about schizophrenia.

On many days I drew him as one of my "bed bath" patients. It wasn't easy rolling him around on the bed and changing the sheets underneath him. His unbroken silence and occasional look of discomfort made it harder.

I always wondered what was happening inside the man's head. Who could really know? Harvey's inscrutable expression always got to me somehow. It suggested an odd combination of Dick Tracy and concentration camp survivor. I decided to try an experiment.

I began talking to the man. No conversation, just a few words each day after checking his reticent pulse. I would shake his hand firmly, lean close, and ask, "How are you doing, Mr. Harvey?"

I continued sending my greeting into the vacuum of his face for about two weeks. He remained incommunicado, but I didn't mind. It felt good just being respectful in this way.

Then one day after I had changed his gown, recorded his temperature, and spoken my greeting, Mr. Harvey looked right at me and mumbled, "How . . . ah . . . you." He squeezed my hand ever so slightly.

I stared back, speechless for the moment, catching a tiny sliver of this man's living personality. I felt as if we'd crossed a great distance and finally met face-to-face. We had our bit of dialogue. I would never be able to regard "non-responsive" patients in the same way again.

Honor that Transforms

In acts of honor we are able to help create each other. That's part of making our religion bigger, our world bigger. We create better things than the meager materials inside most of us might suggest. We nurture personhood. And we are asked to nurture it even in those who hurt us. God tells us to love our enemies and pray for those who misuse us; He can ask this because He did it so well on Golgotha. In Romans 5, Paul reminded his readers that Jesus died for them while they were quite happily sinning against Him. It's rare enough for anyone to give his life for another person; a few heroic types might die for a noble person, but to die for the obnoxious, the ungrateful, the un-promising—that falls off the end of the equation; that's hard honor.

Paul learned it. He could never stand apart in judgment from even the worst. He was always involved because of God's overshad-owing grace. To the Corinthian believers, who'd stumbled over every-thing from bitter lawsuits to incest, he exclaimed, "I do not speak to condemn you; for I have said before that you are in our hearts to die together and to live together." [10] It is this hardest kind of honor which has the most potential of transforming people.

Frank and Elizabeth Morris were driving Tommy back to jail af-ter one of his MADD (Mothers Against Drunk Driving) speaking en-gagements. He began talking about the Bible study course the Morrises had introduced him to and how he felt strengthened by it. Soon it became apparent that the young man had made a commitment to Christ.

Frank asked him, "Have you been baptized?"

"No, but I'd like to be," Tommy answered.

The three were just about to pass the church where the Morrises were members. They pulled into the parking lot and stepped inside. Frank had been authorized to perform baptisms, so he led Tommy up to the front of the sanctuary, draped him in a white robe and waded into the frigid baptismal pool.

As Elizabeth watched her husband raise his arm over Tommy's bowed head she recalled an almost identical scene several years be-fore when Frank had immersed their son Ted in the same pool after his commitment at age 11.

But there was one big difference. Tommy was no earnest adoles-cent, but a convicted killer. And the person he had killed was the Morrises' only son. After drinking himself into a stupor one night in 1982, he'd climbed in his car, swerved down a road and smashed into 18-year-old Ted's car head-on.

The Morrises were, of course, consumed with grief and rage. Frank followed the legal proceedings religiously, living for the day when Tommy would be found guilty and executed. Elizabeth, when not contemplating suicide or crying her heart out on Ted's pillow, fan-tasized about throwing the electric chair switch herself.

Shocked by the depth of her hatred, she began praying for a

way out of it, haunted by Christ's words on the cross: "Father forgive them . . ." One day Tommy spoke at Ted's high school, as part of his rehabilitation, and Elizabeth mustered enough courage to speak to him afterwards. Then, finding that no one ever visited the youth in jail, she decided to go see him. When she spotted this utterly desolate young man through the bars, Elizabeth felt an unexpected surge of warmth.

After a bit Tommy blurted out, "Mrs. Morris . . . I'm so sorry. Please forgive me."

For a moment everything froze as Elizabeth stared at the man. The cruelty of her boy's death was still fresh in her heart. But she also thought of the Father who lost an only Son, of His incredible act of honoring on the cross, and everything became clear. Elizabeth made a decision. She forgave Tommy sincerely and asked his forgiveness for the hatred she'd nurtured for months.

The Morrises had stuck by Tommy, helping him start his rehabilitation. In time they were able to convince him that God could help him fight his alcoholism. However, although Frank had found the strength to help Tommy, he still struggled with forgiving him.

But then came that spontaneous moment of baptism. When Frank lifted Tommy out of the water, the youth begged, "Please, I want you to forgive me, too." He embraced him desperately. Finally this bereaved father could say the words through his tears, "Yes, I forgive you."

Tommy's chances of rehabilitation weren't that good. He bore the psychological handicaps of growing up in a troubled family and had been addicted to alcohol from the age of 16. But he did succeed in finding sobriety, a steady job, and a strong sense of purpose serving the Lord. It happened largely because Elizabeth called him every day with encouraging words. It happened because Tommy's first job on the outside was doing work for Frank around the house. The grieving couple found their way to hard honor. In the end, they counted the killer as their son—and he became a new person. [11]

Chapter Twelve

SPLENDID ROBES AND SPECIAL SERVANTS

We've looked at the epic of honor in Scripture. We've looked at its functional shape in New Testament epistles. Now we turn to the story that the church presents to us in attempting to reflect that quality. It's a story that has special relevance to us today. It's a story that relates to the Advent movement. God's people in the last days are called to bring this story to a climax.

The tradition of honor begins brightly in the first century: "How these Christians love one another!" was the first pagan response (quoted by Tertullian) to the Christian movement. From the very beginning Christians made it a point to honor those least likely to receive benevolent regard. Funds were regularly collected, Tertullian wrote,

> " . . . to feed the poor and bury them, for boys and girls who lack property and parents, and then for slaves grown old and shipwrecked mariners; and any who may be in the mines, on the penal islands, in prison . . . they become the pensioners of the confession." [1]

The good news about God's grace paved the way for a new way of looking at the disadvantaged. They weren't objects of God's curse, but people capable of redemption. Most of the early Christians did an exceptional job of knocking down barriers of class and race that got in the way of honor.

The Emperor Julian, writing to his pagan clergy about the influence of Christians, complained, "The impious Galileans support not only their own poor, but ours as well, everyone can see that our people lack aid from us."[2]

When a severe famine struck the eastern Roman Empire, pagans looked around for someone to blame. They decided that their gods were angry and demanded elimination of the "atheists" in their midst. Yet these followers of Jesus awed everyone by their selfless caring for the victims of famine, pagan and Christian alike.

Women especially benefited from Christian honor. Treated as equals in the eyes of God, they took on important roles in the church. Husbands were told to treat their wives with as much consideration as Christ showed His bride, the church.

It's important to remember that all the lofty ideals we hear about from the philosophers of Greece and Rome applied only to the elite in society. Their ethic was for aristocrats only. But those moved by Christ's honor brought a different social order into the world. They extended grace and dignity to all human beings—even to their most ruthless enemies. The Epistle to Diognetus states, "They love all men, and are persecuted by all. . . . They are poor, and make many rich. They lack everything, and in everything they abound . . . They are abused—and they bless. They are reviled, and are justified. They are insulted, and they repay insults with honour."[3]

Some Christians under torture would not reveal their name or social class, home or place of origin. They simply said they were Christians who belonged to a universal church, and refused to claim any other identity.

Delivered from Blindness

Toward the end of the fourth century the fifteen-year-old son of wealthy property owners in Britain was captured by Irish pirates and taken up to Ireland. There he labored as a slave tending sheep. After six years, he managed to escape and made his way back home, with great difficulty and providential help.

His experience in captivity had been quite a shock to the lad. Before, he'd known only a sheltered life on his father's comfortable estate. You wouldn't expect him to express any fondness for those bandits up north who had enslaved him during the best years of his youth. And yet this boy, Patrick, ended up spending his life in Ireland, laboring to bring its people from paganism to Christianity.

During his years of captivity, Patrick had discovered God as a very present Helper in times of trouble. Apparently he'd been quite indifferent to religious matters before, but in Ireland he'd begun fervently worshiping his Lord. Later he would look back on those six years not as tragic captivity but as a great deliverance from spiritual blindness. Patrick wrote in his *CONFESSION:* "Before I was humiliated I was like a stone that lies in deep mud, and he who is mighty came and in his compassion raised me up and exalted me very high and placed me on the top of the wall."[4]

The experience of finding in God a deliverer, both physical and spiritual, when no human help was available, gave Patrick a profound appreciation of redemption; it made justification by faith graphic. And so when the call came to minister in Ireland, Patrick went, propelled by hard honor. Those people up north weren't just barbarians who had enslaved him, they were individuals whose lives had been rendered invaluable by the shed blood of Christ. Patrick set off to become a good shepherd for the redeemable.

For a time the gospel-proclaiming church did bring a whole new way of honoring human beings into the world. But gradually other kinds of honor crept in which compromised the principle of seeing every human being primarily through Christ's act of honor. Virginity became something of a status symbol in the church, a higher level of spirituality that the married could not attain. All the glory of mystical union with Christ, which every believer is entitled to, was focused on the cult of virginity. Many church leaders believed that only the celibate could be spiritual in the deepest sense.

Others who had suffered persecution and torture for their faith also came to occupy an upper niche in the church. "The confessors" sometimes lorded it over other members, and most occupied prominent positions. Less distinguished believers bowed before their heroic accomplishments.

It's commendable, of course, to admire those who suffer for their faith and those who forgo marriage in order to dedicate themselves to Christian service. But when they attained a certain exclusive status in the body of Christ, then hard honor is fractured. The old honor of coats-of-arms and titles and privileges has crept in.

During the Middle Ages, the work of extending the gospel, and thus Christ's honor, didn't occupy center stage. Honor was further compromised by the increasingly high status of the clergy. Those who made that mystical sacrifice of Christ's body during Mass took on cosmic size above their congregations. Believers were obliged to pay homage to men in splendid robes and also to holy relics in splendid shrines. The outward trappings of holiness took the focus away from more redeemable inner qualities.

But there were still radicals around during this time who majored in honor as a verb.

While riding through the plain below the town of Assisi, a youth named Francis encountered a leper and was horrified by the man's appearance. But, determined to be a knight of Christ, he slipped off his horse and ran toward the man who extended his palm to receive some alms. Francis gave him a few coins—and a kiss.

Later, according to Bonaventure, Francis would live with a group of lepers for a time "serving them all most diligently for God's sake. He washed their feet, bandaged their ulcers, drew the pus from their wounds." [5]

There were quite a few saints who took on the challenge of Christ's honor in earnest. Joan of Orveito's contemporaries used to say, "Anyone who wants Sister Joan's prayers should do her a bad turn."

Ignatius walked many miles out of his way in winter to nurse a man he heard had fallen ill—the same man who'd stolen Ignatius's small store of money a few weeks before.

Saint Spiridion interrupted a gang of thieves attempting to make off with his sheep one night, but set them free with a gift of a ram, "Lest they should have been up all night for nothing."

More Room

The Reformation pushed out considerable more room for honor. It championed the priesthood of believers and spotlighted its theological source: justification by faith. But in the fierce battles over this and other doctrines, honor was often trampled. Theological opponents did not often seem redeemable, especially when they remained unmoved by your arguments.

The circle of honor did not yet include Jews. Protestant preachers could wax eloquent about the Christ who opened his arms to those who remained indifferent to his sacrifice, the One who would not curse even those who mocked it. But many in the church called for harsh penalties against the Hebrews who remained indifferent in the present.

Some in the Reformed tradition began to draw sharp lines between the elect and those not elected, the chosen and those on the outside. Puritan preaching at times implied that the poor were undeserving—after all, God had made them poor. Those who prospered economically took success as a sign of God's blessing—and election. Eventually, only upstanding, hard-working citizens could claim the possibility of redemption. In many Christian minds, God was no longer looking for an opportunity to save, but working rigidly through the machine of predestination.

By the nineteenth century, Christ's honor had been watered down into middle-class respectability. Charles Spurgeon's peers could draw boundaries between themselves and the unwashed masses. William Booth could not. His Salvation Army regulars, like Spurgeon's Tabernacle volunteers, sought out the unlikeliest candidates of grace in the slums of the industrial revolution.

The great revivals of the eighteenth and nineteenth centuries created an awakening of Christ's honor and gave birth to the modern missionary movement. Unfortunately, some missionaries allied themselves with imperialism and the political interests of their home country. They did not honor, but patronized, and sometimes exploited. But those most propelled by the gospel, like the Moravians, were the most likely to truly honor the peoples they worked among and look for aspects of their culture that were redeemable.

There have been extraordinarily sensitive missionaries who upheld Christ's honor, like David Brainerd among the American Indians, Adoniram Judson among the Burmese, Hudson Taylor among the Chinese and, in the twentieth century, Don Richardson among the Sawi people of Irian Jaya. Richardson discovered a cannibalistic culture that had somehow developed an ethic of crafty betrayal and murder as its highest ideal. But he still found something to honor among the Sawi: their concept of a Peace Child. And it was that part of Sawi culture which he made blossom into the hard honor of Christ.

Honor has had its skillful champions at home too, like Paul Tournier, the Swiss physician who was among the first to minister to the whole person. He left a remarkable record of healing. Patients came to him with a wide range of physical and psychological problems. He brought many to health and wholeness by sharing good medicine and also personal wisdom from his own devotional life. Tournier consistently reached into psyches twisted by neurotic guilt and bitterness, and touched something redeemable.

We also see a wonderful kind of honor in the ministry of an Albanian nun named Mother Teresa who labored cheerfully among the poorest of the poor in Calcutta. She chose to concentrate on those least likely to win assistance in a bottomless ocean of poverty where only a few promising souls could normally be rescued. Mother Teresa cared for the destitute and dying. She and her sisters (the Missionaries of Charity) walked through the slums in their blue and white saris each day to pick up emaciated bodies lying in the street. They took these poor souls back to a shelter where they could die with a measure of dignity, assured of God's love, surrounded by gentle hands, looking up at a smiling human face.

Teresa's work didn't follow the prescription of triage. It had no great economic impact or strategic value. It was a work of art. As Teresa would describe it, "a beautiful work for God." But her ministry has become one of the most powerful statements made in the twentieth century. Hard honor. Mother Teresa expressed it so well because she saw much more than disease-ridden, filthy bodies amid the refuse of Calcutta. She saw Jesus in disguise, the One who said, "Whatever you did for one of the least of these brothers of mine, you did for me."

This Albanian nun really did feel she was touching Christ when she caressed some nameless face brought in off the streets barely breathing. She once wrote this prayer for herself:

> Dearest Lord, may I see you today and every day in
> the person of your sick, and, whilst nursing them, minister
> unto you. Though you hide yourself behind the unattractive
> disguise of the irritable, the exacting, the unreasonable, may

I still recognize you, and say: "Jesus, my patient, how sweet it is to serve you."[6]

The Arms of the Father

A small group of Americans and Auca Indians gathered at dawn on a sand bar of the Curaray River deep in the rain forest of Ecuador. Kimo, an Auca pastor, began explaining the meaning of baptism to four teenagers, Steve and Kathy Saint and two Auca youths. He reminded them that their immersion in the water was a witness of the death and resurrection of Christ.

As the low, fiery tropical sun cast long shadows, Rachel Saint watched her nephew and niece file into the river. Her brother Nate could not be there to share in the event. He had bled to death on this sand bar some years before when his kids were small. Four other missionaries had died with him, speared by a group of Aucas which included Kimo. The man who stood now in the Curaray raising his hand solemnly over fourteen-year-old Steve had once raised his weapon against the boy's father and helped kill him as the missionary held his hands high, pleading for mercy.

Nate Saint had been longing for some time to reach the isolated, greatly feared Aucas. In 1667, a Jesuit priest had attempted to introduce the faith to Aucaland and been quickly dispatched. Two hundred years later, rubber hunters entered the forest and burned Auca homes, raped the women, and killed or enslaved the men. The Aucas had reason to be unneighborly.

But Nate and his companions began dropping gifts to the Aucas from an airplane. They called out friendly phrases and got a few smiles and waves in response. Finally they decided to chance a face-to-face encounter and selected a sand bar they nicknamed Palm Beach for a landing. The men knew it was risky. One of the group, Jim Elliot, told his wife, "If that's the way God wants it to be, I'm ready to die for the salvation of the Aucas."

All the signs had been good, but something went wrong during that first encounter between Kimo and his companions and the missionaries. The Indians' deeply rooted fear that foreigners came only to kill and destroy compelled them to shed blood.

Remarkably enough, the missionary widows did not beat a hasty retreat from what most would regard as a land of savages. They remained in Ecuador with their children and continued attempts to reach tribes in the forest. These women had a hold on a hard honor that insisted against the odds that these people were redeemable.

Eventually, an Auca girl who'd left the tribe after her father was killed was converted and went back to her people to tell them about Jesus and His great sacrifice. One month later, Rachel Saint and Elizabeth Elliot hung their hammocks with the Aucas. They began living out their forgiveness day after day in the Indian village and pointing to its source in the atonement of Christ. Kimo was one of the first to see in Christ's blood a means of spiritual cleansing.

And so they'd come to this dawn on the banks of the Curaray. Those two fatherless teenagers also knew about hard honor. They had something to express. Kathy and Steve Saint had made their own decision about who would baptize them. They'd chosen Kimo as the one who would usher them symbolically into the arms of a Heavenly Father.

After the baptism, Rachel Saint and Kimo and the four teenagers walked over to the graves of the five martyrs. Together they sang the hymn that those five men had sung just before departing to meet their fate:

> We rest on Thee, our Shield and our Defender
> Thine is the battle, Thine shall be the praise
> When passing through the gates of pearly splendor
> Victors, we rest with Thee through endless days. [7]

These are masterpieces of honor, artful goodness at its best. They belong on large canvases dominating our gallery walls. They embody the act of atonement, the will to mercy. They make it real and vivid over the world's small landscape of tepid loves and gaudy hates.

It's only fitting that Rachel and Steve Saint's act of art, like that of Frank and Elizabeth Morris, involves the rite of baptism. In baptism a new believer accepts a wildly improbable honor: identification with Christ's heroic death and resurrection. He is re-titled, re-clothed, re-counted as a person with all the rights and privileges of the Beloved Son who marched confidently into heaven and into God's throne room after a triumphal tour de force on earth.

The Saint family managed to honor other people as they had been honored by God. That's the primary ethical thrust of the New Testament, it's a call to arms that echoes beneath all other admonitions. Hard honor anchors us to God's act of atonement, that greatest of artistic spectacles played out on a hilltop against dark rolling clouds, flashes of thunder, earthquake and a large cast playing humanity at its best and worst. We must express that act, flesh it out. We must make our own canvases out of the atonement.

This is our heritage as artists of the Spirit. We can learn from the way believers have tried to express the grace of Christ down through history. They leave us a gallery of canvases, some plain, some badly composed, some achingly beautiful. How can we build on this tradition? How can we make our religion bigger?

The three angels flying down from heaven who've been entrusted with final warning messages for this world are propelled by one primary message: the everlasting gospel of Jesus Christ. Their urgent admonitions are given in the light of God's extraordinary grace, in the light of the Cross.

Hard honor is our best expression of what that divine sacrifice really means. It's how we embody it in our lives. It's how we make it visible for the spiritually hungry people around us.

We have the challenge of fleshing out Christ's honor in our present world. We must always get our bearings and our inspiration from the hard honor given clear shape in the New Testament. But all those who have gone before us also urge us on to express that eternal quality, to create something new out of it that will be compelling for our contemporaries.

Chapter Thirteen

AFRAID OF A
PLACE TO STAND

The leaders of the Khmer Rouge looked out over Cambodian rice fields and felt a need to do something about the chronic poverty of their countrymen. Pockets of wealth among the merchants and officials in the capital city of Phnom Penh seemed to produce only decadence. So the Khmer Rouge chose socialism as their solution. They refined communist doctrines into an urgent mandate for immediate change that they called "pure revolution."

Beginning in 1975, they began implementing their truth. The Khmer Rouge turned Cambodian society upside down. They emptied the capital and drove its inhabitants out to the countryside to work in communal farms. Everyone would be equal. No more exploitation. No more city decadence.

But the pure revolution required the sacrifice of those who couldn't be pressed quickly enough into the new mold, and there were many who erred against the Khmer Rouge program. Farms run by soldiers of the regime turned into killing fields where millions of uprooted Cambodian men, women and children starved or were executed. The new era of absolute equality dawned among vast pyramids of skulls. When news first leaked out about the number of casualties, it seemed preposterous, most people couldn't fathom a tragedy so vast in the name of reform.

Iran's Shi'ite Moslems felt a growing need in the '70s to somehow fight against the decadence of the West that was tearing many of their countrymen from the faith of their fathers. Iran's powerful Shah had brought some measure of prosperity to the country, but his policies also produced unwanted side effects: increased alcoholism, drug abuse, prostitution, and a general turning away from God to materialism. Time for reform.

Led by the Ayatollah Khomeini, Moslem fundamentalists created a revolution in 1979, bringing the nation back to faith, truth, and morality. Iranians gathered in enthusiastic crowds around their new charismatic, authoritative leader. They kept chanting slogans feverishly until these became an all-enveloping truth.

Tehran was cleaned up. No more addicted teenage girls roaming the streets. Far fewer drunk husbands carousing with other women on weekends.

But the new morality required constant enforcement: Revolutionary Guards roaming the cities began checking up on women not covered from head to toe. An exposed lock of hair or rolled-up sleeve warranted a lecture or even arrest; repeat offenders were beaten.

Eventually, the Ayatollah's moral revolution required the sacrifice of countless enemies. There were many summary trials and executions of nonconformists. One of the familiar sayings plastered on buildings in every city read: "Whoever fights against the truth shall be defeated." Truth had to be defended at all costs. Its enemies were everywhere. America, that old exporter of decadence, became Satan. A troublesome neighbor like Iraq was transformed into the embodiment of evil and Khomeini declared a holy war against it. Turbanned mullah clergymen promoted martyrdom among teenage boys. These youth become fervent BASIJ, volunteers who were often asked in battle to form a human wave moving ahead of regular soldiers to distract the enemy and clear the ground of mines.

Defending the pure faith required a fountain of blood. There was an reminder of that in the town of Mashhad; at its center stood a three-tiered fountain bubbling water dyed a deep red. Behind it loomed a portrait of the Ayatollah, and below him photographs of his many loyal dead.

Aching, Yet Afraid

It's no wonder that people these days are very gun-shy about anyone shouting for one truth, one faith, and calling for absolute allegiance. Behind those who take the strongest stands against evil, we seem to always see the shadow of the guillotine. Those willing to die for the truth are usually willing to kill for it too. That's scary. Many of our contemporaries have decided that maybe it's better just to keep absolute truth out of the picture. Maybe we should scale down our allegiances to something more manageable.

What I feel. What I believe. What I like. Those seem less dangerous objectives in our world, and many have adopted them with relief and even a sense of self-righteousness. They won't talk too loudly about right and wrong. The circle of truth is confined to ME.

But sometimes the world aches for someone to take a stand and declare a great allegiance. Evil is still out there and its victims multiply. At times human silence can seem painfully loud. Almost none of the Germans in the 1940s who passed by columns of starving, ragged Jewish fellow countrymen marching off to death camps took a stand against Nazi authority. They would not ask questions. They averted their gaze from the hollow eyes and sunken cheeks. This was not happening to them; it was not their responsibility.

Almost none of the white people in the 50s who passed by ramshackle schoolhouses where African Americans were forced to try to educate their children took a stand against the hallowed tradition of segregation. This was not happening to THEIR children. Their well-defined circle of ME did not include those of another color.

People find it hard to make stands against evils that aren't happening to them. We find it hard to oppose lies that are not about us. But declaring our allegiance to the truth, making a stand against evil is essential in our world. We don't live in a garden where we can wander about picking any old flower and simply enjoy the fragrance of whatever we feel, whatever we choose to believe. Thorns are everywhere. Cruelty and human suffering abound. Our kids grow up in a sea of drugs, our culture is awash in violence. Teenagers can't just drift; they'll drown if they do; they have to resist at some point.

The same holds true for any of us—from the televangelist stretching the truth in his fundraising letter to the nurse who refuses to care for an AIDS patient. Stands against the tide are essential, not optional.

People making stands keep our head above water. We have to declare some higher allegiance in order for evil not to completely dominate us. We can't drift. Without making a stand, we're more amoebas than human beings.

When you get right down to it, it's a bit frightening to think there's no truth on the horizon bigger than our individual selves. We are constantly urged to "find your truth," and assured that ultimate answers and god are found in some inner recess of the heart; it's all within you. I don't find that very comforting. In a world where truth has no separate existence, it's almost impossible to make courageous stands. How can anyone be expected to make sacrifices? There's nothing more important than me out there.

And yet most of the stands against evil we see in the world aren't that comforting either. Belligerent crowds chanting out their fanatical allegiances, revolutionaries devising some pure doctrine that justifies genocide, forces like these turn truth into a bloodthirsty threat.

That's the dilemma people face in our world. We need to give allegiance to something bigger than ourselves, and yet don't want to be swept away by it. We ache for a meaningful place to make a stand in the world, and are afraid of finding it.

Can Adventists show others a way out of that dilemma? Can we show them a meaningful alternative?

Fortunately our church has a strong tradition emphasizing the separation of church and state. We are keenly away of the dangers of coercive religion. We have an eye on end-time events when the antichrist power will attempt to legislate conformity to false doctrine. Adventists believe in freedom of conscience.

We have this big picture of a God who will not force His truth on the world. A God who labors patiently through the ages to work out His plan of salvation. A God who vows to use only one instrument to win human hearts and minds, and that's the instrument of selfless love.

The question is how can we live out that big picture in our daily lives? How can we show it in the way we take stands against evil? How can we show the world a kind of allegiance to truth that will prove winsome instead of frightening?

I believe that's part of our calling. We've been blessed with wonderful truths to share. Those truths give people a better picture of our heavenly Father. Now we need to demonstrate something more, something about the way we bear witness to the truth. The way we take a stand on principles sometimes speaks louder than the principles we stand on.

We need to demonstrate an allegiance of a very special kind in order to win the world to God's truth. We need to show that the truth doesn't turn us into fanatics, doesn't make us want to coerce others, doesn't constrict our lives.

In order to get a handle on the good kind of allegiance, allegiance as a virtue, let's go back to our roots as Protestant believers. We'll find a wonderful starting point in a man who made a historic stand for principle—against all the odds.

Treasury of Merit

Europe in the beginning of the Sixteenth Century badly needed someone to take a stand. Unfortunately, the very church that had unified society in the Middle Ages seemed to make a meaningful allegiance impossible. Christendom had been corrupted from the top down. By most accounts, negligence, ignorance, absenteeism, and sexual immorality plagued the clergy. They had become a privileged class wielding cosmic power over the laity. Warrior Pope Julius II went on a series of ventures which required a ghastly shedding of blood. His successor, Pope Leo X, earned this description from one historian: "elegant and as indolent as a Persian cat. His chief pre-eminence lay in his ability to squander the resources of the Holy See on carnivals, war, gambling, and the chase."

The church clenched the keys to the kingdom tightly. It threatened the unruly, gullible masses with the power to excommunicate. It dictated truth, jealously guarding its exclusive right to read and interpret the Scriptures. It amassed wealth, coming to rival the states of Europe in its temporal power.

Interestingly enough, almost everyone acknowledged clerical abuses and the sorry state of religious life. Many voices raised the cry for reform. But no one could find the leverage to move a colossal religious power off its vested interests. The basic problem was that Rome profited immensely from the "mechanical religion" into which Christianity had degenerated.

Rome's corporate portfolio included a piece of Moses' burning bush, the chains of St. Paul, and St. Veronica's napkin with a portrait of Christ. These and countless other hot properties created a great treasury of merit which could be drawn upon by the many pilgrims visiting the holy city. One of the coins paid to Judas for betraying Christ held great potential merit; it had been ruled that a visit to that relic alone could result in 1400 years taken off someone's sentence in Purgatory. Crawling up Pilate's Stairs, the Scala Sancta, on hands and knees while repeating a Pater Noster at each step could release a soul from limbo outright.

By the sixteenth century, the accumulated merit of the saints, available through such relics and rituals, had been quantified as indulgences. Receiving an indulgence meant that this merit from the surplus fund could be transferred to some needy sinner with a meager account.

Moment of Truth

In 1510, two monks were sent to Rome to consult with the Pope and settle a dispute that had arisen in their Augustinian order. One of the monks was named Martin Luther. He considered it a wonderful privilege to be able to visit the Eternal City. Here was a grand opportunity to appropriate the enormous spiritual benefits available. Luther set out to celebrate Mass at sacred shrines, visit the catacombs and basilicas, venerate the bones of martyrs, pray at their shrines, and adore as many holy relics as possible.

But slowly this monk became disillusioned. The Italian priests he met seemed almost flippant about their duties. He was shocked by stories of gross immorality among the clergy; some considered themselves virtuous because they confined themselves to women.

At that point, this lone monk in a vast city of holy places began to doubt. He wondered whether a sacred shrine or relic could actually convey merit. Luther was climbing up Pilate's stairs on his hands and knees, repeating the Lord's Prayer at every step and kissing each one, when suddenly, having arrived at the top, he raised himself and exclaimed, "Who knows whether it is so?"

Martin Luther had come up against the elaborate system of merit earning which greased the wheels of the church—and he found it wanting. At first his doubt was only a despairing thought: if these means of merit prescribed by the church could not really bestow grace, what hope was there?

In response to this moment of truth, Luther could have dropped back into cynicism, exploiting the institution he no longer believed in, like so many of his contemporaries. Instead he continued to anguish through six-hour confessions, feverish good works and penitence in search of some assurance of acceptance with the holy God.

And he finally found it—after he was assigned to the chair of Bible at the University of Wittenberg. He began studying and lecturing on the book of Psalms and discovered many verses foreshadowing the life and death of the Redeemer. Luther's thoughts turned more and more to the Christ who takes on himself our iniquity. Then he studied Paul's Epistle to the Romans and there discovered the truth of justification by faith.

Suddenly Luther felt all the excitement of a man beholding a new continent. The justice of God, that had always seemed a terrifying obstacle, now reshaped itself into "the just shall live by faith." Luther wrote: "I grasped that the justice of God is that righteousness by which through grace and sheer mercy God justifies us through faith. Thereupon I felt myself to be reborn and to have gone through open doors into paradise. The whole of Scripture took on a new meaning. . . ."

A Time to Speak

For Luther, Paul's gospel threw a sharp light on the mechanical Christianity around him. One day an indulgence-vendor named Tetzel paraded into town. He was preceded by dignitaries, a cross emblazoned with the papal arms, and a bull of indulgence carried on a gold-embroidered velvet cushion. Tetzel planted the cross in the market place and proclaimed that a special indulgence had been issued by his Holiness in order to defray the expense of rebuilding St. Peter's basilica. Subscribers would enjoy a complete and perfect remission of all their sins.

The time had come to speak. Luther did so, on the eve of All Saints Day, by posting a proposal to debate ninety-five theses on the door of the Castle Church in Wittenberg. They proved to be of more than academic interest. The Augustinian professor's theses were secretly translated from Latin into German, passed on to the press, and soon became the hot topic in Germany.

People had protested against financial exploitation like Tetzel's for over a century without much to show for it. But Luther was able to strike a more resounding blow. Carried along by the momentum of his new-found allegiance to justification by faith, he blasted indulgences as a blasphemy against the mercy of God. He declared that the saints have no surplus of holy credit to bestow and affirmed that Christ's "merits are freely available without the keys of the pope."

Pope Leo X heard about these dangerous views and quickly decided to "smother the fire before it should become a conflagration." He first exerted pressure on Luther's Augustinian order to have him censured. But at their triennial gathering in Heidelberg, the professor of Bible defended himself quite effectively.

His enemies began to boast that he would burn within a month. But Luther didn't budge. This was a painfully sensitive monk who'd spent years groveling after deeper penance, continually begging his superiors for some additional burden of good deeds. But now he'd found a place to stand. Clinging to the rock of the gospel in order to save himself, he'd found, quite unexpectedly, enormous leverage. He discovered the strength to face down the whole medieval system of legalism.

While church authorities threatened, Luther kept studying, and was further radicalized. He noticed that Jesus call to "Repent" in Matthew 4:17 was translated in the Latin as "do penance." But Erasmus's Greek New Testament showed the original had the sense of "be penitent," literally, "change your mind." This undercut the church's highly evolved sacrament of penitence.

Threatened with excommunication, something that always paralyzed medieval individuals with fear, Luther calmly replied, "Only God can sever spiritual communion. No creature can separate us from the love of Christ."

When a Dominican named Prierias issued an official written reply to Luther's views which emphasized the authority of the Universal Church, the Reformer wrote back with words that would become his most telling protest: "You cite no Scripture. You give no reasons."

Luther made the same simple protest in a debate with John Eck at the University of Leipzig. During the long and heated discussion Eck accused his opponent of "espousing the pestilent errors of John Hus" the Bohemian heretic burned at the stake. Luther took the opportunity to speak on behalf of an authoritative Word and human conscience: "No believing Christian can be coerced beyond holy writ. By divine law we are forbidden to believe anything which is not established by divine

Scripture or manifested revelation."

Eck pressed Luther with an attack others had frequently repeated: "Are you the only one that knows anything? Except for you is all the Church in error?" It is difficult for us today to understand how powerfully that argument must have struck the Augustinian professor. The Church had been for him mother and conscience and truth. It made the world coherent. Luther was still profoundly devoted to it; he did not wish to be a schismatic. But he could not fall back among the countless other would-be reformers who'd become part of the exploitative, legalistic system. He could not forget his allegiance to those many clear testimonies from Scripture. No one had refuted them. And so he told Eck that he had to confess his convictions, that he was willing to defend the truth with his blood, and that, after all, "God once spoke through the mouth of an ass."

In between debates and the complicated legal maneuvers that kept him ahead of the stake, Luther put together a thorough program of reform in an "Address to the German Nobility." He called for an end to clerical elitism: All believers should have the same legal rights. He objected to the pope's exclusive claim to interpret Scripture. Didn't the Bible promise that any lay person could understand the mind of Christ? He wanted the papacy to curtail its vast income-generating machine and rediscover apostolic simplicity.

Again and again Luther contrasted the corruption and decadence of church leaders with the humble servanthood of Christ. Luther's call succeeded in shaking Europe out of its complacency. Many people finally sat up and took notice of the radically different ideal for the church apparent in God's Word. However, those protecting their power dug in their heels. Luther's books were publicly burned in Rome and a bull condemning him was disseminated.

Luther still stood firm, issuing his trademark reply: "This bull condemns me from its own word without any proof from Scripture. . . ."

Here I Stand

The big showdown occurred before an imperial assembly at Worms. The setting is justly famous. Enthroned in pomp and splendor sat Charles, the Holy Roman Emperor, glorious symbol of all the medieval unities, culmination of a line of legendary Catholic sovereigns going back to Charlemagne. Around him were representatives of papal power in their imposing robes. And before them all stood a former monk, a tin miner's son, without a shred of authority, but with a growing faith in the sufficiency of God's Word.

Luther did not come before his chief examiner, the Archbishop of Trier, cockily. When first asked whether he would repudiate his writings, his reply was barely audible. But Luther's reticence was due less to the august assembly than to his conviction that all present stood before Almighty God and must give answer to Him. Later, in a speech explaining the purpose behind his various published works, Luther found his voice. He spoke for the many in Northern Europe who now struggled to reform the church fundamentally: "Universal complaints testify that by the laws of the popes the consciences of men are racked."

"No!" the emperor interposed.

Luther went on unruffled, "When Christ stood before Annas, he said, 'Produce witnesses.' If our Lord, who could not err, made this demand, why may not a worm like me ask to be convicted of error from the prophets and the Gospels? If I am shown my error, I will be the first to throw my books into the fire."

The archbishop asserted that Luther had no right to call into question "the most holy orthodox faith" confirmed by "sacred councils" and "so many famous men." Then he demanded, "Do you not repudiate your books and the errors which they contain?"

Asked to choose between certain death and the betrayal of what he saw as the plain, repeated teaching of Scripture, Luther chose the former. "Unless I am convicted by Scripture and plain reason—I do not accept the authority of popes and councils . . . my conscience is captive to the Word of God . . . Here I stand, I cannot do otherwise."[1]

Here is a picture to remember. Before the pageantry and ceremony of medieval authority, one man stood as an iron wedge lifting it off dead center—a plain, thick-featured wedge driven against a colossus which wielded non-negotiable decree and inquisition. This man declared his unconditional allegiance and as a result Christendom tumbled over into reformation.

Luther was not a particularly elegant artist of the spirit. It's his persistence against the odds that makes the picture striking. Out of the monolithic stone of medieval authority, he carved out a place for an individual believer enlightened by God's Word. He kept presenting the truth of the gospel against all that would distort it, until finally its own authority broke through.

Chapter Fourteen

INTO THE CLUTCHES
OF THE WORLD

Martin Luther shows us a wonderful kind of allegiance. It was an allegiance to the moral authority of Scripture. That's where he found the leverage to resist human decrees backed by the sword. That's the place where he made a meaningful stand against evil. In the Word, people can find a Truth big enough to overshadow self-interest.

This Is It

The Bible compels. Even individuals who run into the Word out of the blue are often captured by the way it speaks with authority. I discovered that while teaching Bible classes in Japan. Most of the college students and young professionals in our English school had no reference points for a personal, transcendent God. They were thoroughly secular. Yet when they did wander into Bible classes to practice English, many were caught by the Word. Its truths had an unexpectedly winsome power. They couldn't easily shake off its call to goodness. I saw totally unprepared individuals fall into the clutches of this authority. And those who did willfully turn away from it, often found it quite difficult to live outside its truths—even though they'd done so rather comfortably before.

The Word packs quit a punch. Sometimes its big, all-inclusive Truth hits people instantly. A Japanese youth walked into an evangelistic meeting and heard Christ's words: "A new commandment I give you: Love one another. As I have loved you, so you must love one another."[1] He immediately made a life-changing commitment: "This is it, this is everything I've been looking for."

A young Jewish intellectual sat reading a New Testament for the first time, wedged among chickens, turkeys and singing passengers in steerage aboard a ship plying the Mediterranean. He got caught up in the drama of Jesus clashing with the Pharisees over a woman caught in adultery. His pulse quickened as the Pharisees pushed Jesus up against the wall with the law demanding this woman's death. For a moment Arthur Katz paused, wondering what Jesus could possibly say in return, and then read the words, "Let him without sin cast the first stone." Katz gasped: "A sword had been plunged deep into my being. It was numbing, shocking, yet thrilling because the answer was so utterly perfect. . . . It cut across every major issue I had ever anguished upon in my life. . . . I knew that what I had read transcended human knowledge and comprehension. It had to be Divine."[2]

The Word strikes deep because it is God speaking, not just nice religious literature. It presents itself as God-breathed, inspired revelation, the will of God. It comes to us from outside, from an absolute perspective; that is why it speaks with authority.

The Word is a compelling force; events are said to occur in order that it may be fulfilled; history is ushered into shape before it. Scripture, the "living and active" Word, has to happen. It is not a suggestion, an option, a possible scenario; it is divine necessity penetrating the artless, formless world. If human beings fail to give it expression, the very rocks will cry out.

Two Kinds of Allegiance

If we relate honestly to this kind of compelling Word, we are inspired to something I call *open allegiance*. We are moved to open ourselves completely before its claims; we want God's voice echoing in our innermost selves. We give the Word our unconditional loyalty—willing to listen to whatever it says and go wherever it clearly directs. Open allegiance presents a whole human being to the whole Word.

However if we present only a piece of ourselves to the Word, or listen only to an agreeable portion of it, we fall into something called *closed allegiance.* We assume we already have all the truth. The subject is closed. We select some pet point of view and cling tightly to it as if it were the whole. We close off other perspectives in the Word and build detours around them. Closed allegiance attempts to box in God's voice instead of broadening it.

The book of Revelation begins with a word of blessing to all who read its words and take them to heart. It ends with a stern warning to those who would delete any of its passages. The Word is not to be played with; it exists to speak to us, not we to it.

A Word we manipulate is no help at all in a world aching for a meaningful allegiance. If we filter everything through our own likes and dislikes then we rob Scripture of its power to enlighten. And this often happens subconsciously. We may think we're taking a stand on the Word of God, but we're really just using it to back up our own opinions. We only see *our* texts. We pass right by the ones that "don't fit." As a result, the Word can't act as revelation. We remain safe in our sphere of closed allegiance. Paul warned Timothy about such a state in which people can no longer stomach "sound doctrine" and gather round likable teachers who tickle their ears with undemanding fables.

But God's Word arrives on the scene as (to re-apply a theologian's phrase) the Wholly Other. When presenting the gospel, Paul insisted: "I did not receive it from any man, nor was I taught it; rather, I received it by revelation from Jesus Christ."[3] Peter broadened the point: "For it was not through any human whim that men prophesied of old; men they were, but, impelled by the Holy Spirit, they spoke the words of God."[4] The prophets passed on messages that sometimes only future generations would comprehend, profound truths which "even angels long to look into."

To the Rescue

Open allegiance expresses the fact that Scripture is bigger than me. "All Scripture is God-breathed and is useful for teaching, rebuking, correcting and training in righteousness."[5] That transcendent Word comes close to correct and reprove. Open allegiance accepts this divine direction. It is willing to have the Word come in and upset things, even favorite habits or cherished notions. Open allegiance listens when the Word becomes a sword of the Spirit battling against evil, even when the blows fall close to home.

This is true of individuals. This is true of a church body. It's not difficult for religious groups to get stuck in a kind of closed allegiance. Adventists have struggled with this problem. Being blessed with doctrinal insights is a good thing. Being given a great controversy perspective that gives a shape to all of history is a wonderful thing. But assuming that you've now discovered all truth as a church is not. Assuming that there is nothing more to learn is dangerous. It's stifling. It's closed allegiance. It boxes in the Word of God.

The Word must speak to us from outside the self-supporting echo of our own culture. We need to be surprised sometimes. And sometimes it's believers from other churches who can make us aware of truths in Scripture that we've overlooked. They can help us see past our blind spots; just as we can help them see past theirs.

Scripture asks of us an open allegiance. It asks us to progress in our understanding of truth. That's much more important than using Scripture to draw lines about who's in and who's out, about who has the real package of doctrinal goods and who doesn't. It's much more valuable to track down facets of the truth we haven't seen before than to track down "enemies of the truth."

Jesus once told a group of Pharisees trying to intimidate Him with their Sons-of-Abraham credentials that they were sons of someone else. They were trying to kill Him because "you have no room for my word," and that they refused to believe Him precisely because He was telling the truth. They shied away from the light because their deeds were evil. The prophet Zechariah once lamented those who had to make their hearts "hard as flint" in order not to absorb the oracles of the Lord Almighty.

The Word itself pushes people one way or another. It is a double-edged sword cutting to the marrow, "to the dividing of soul and spirit" where we make moral choices affecting our destiny. Sometimes we think we can wield that sword pretty confidently as we cut away at "doctrinal error" in others. But the primary work of this Sword of the Spirit is to deal with issues in our own hearts.

The Truth is not quite as amiable a guest as we in the safety of the "true church" often assume. It does not politely step around all our cherished furniture and sit down only where directed. When taken to heart as the Word of God, it can wreak havoc, overturning our pet theories, piercing our best defenses. The Word has the authority to arrest us even in the privacy of our own "sincere beliefs" and shove us out into that light which the Pharisees found so threatening.

Special Kind of Authority

Open allegiance is a response to that specific kind of authority. It is very different from, say, truth by acclamation. It is, in fact, the opposite of the crowd chanting slogans and claiming the authority of the guillotine. A close look at the Word itself shows us why.

We start with the prophets. The dominant picture they present is simple moral authority cast against the corruption of Israel's king or priest or people. They were lone, often lonely, voices crying out in an idolatrous darkness. Usually they were ignored or censured; some were beaten, thrown into pits, dismembered. The great majority possessed no official position, no legal or military leverage, nothing except an earnest "Thus sayeth the Lord." That was how they made a stand and hoped to change society.

When we come to Christ, the picture crystallizes. Christ above all "spoke as one having authority."[6] How? By lining up a squadron of Roman soldiers behind Him? By negotiating for a Sanhedrin endorsement? No. By piercing men's hearts with the Truth. His words compelled. He is the quintessential Word and the quintessential reformer. He appeared to be only a meek rabbi badly in need of some political or social clout. But in fact He swayed great multitudes just with the power of His Word.

The apostles, animated by Jesus' Spirit, carried on that tradition. Paul was careful even to refrain from using eloquent oratory to manipulate his hearers. He believed he was called to present the gospel "not with words of human wisdom, lest the cross of Christ be emptied of its power."[7] He and all his colleagues made a stand before Jew and pagan, before influential priest and autocratic Roman ruler, wielding only one thing: the gospel. No other defense, no other support, no other authority. They simply sought to win people to the Word.

Any other kind of authority betrays the real one. The minute people start manipulating or coercing others to enforce truth they deny the authority of the Word. They assert that human beings must be compelled by some other means. They cut themselves off from the voice of prophet, apostle, and Christ. This is closed allegiance—fastening on some piece of the Word as a club instead of encouraging others to open up before it.

The Word of God can certainly be misused. Its words have been quoted to justify all kinds of practices that hurt human beings or war against the truth. So some suggest that we water down its authority a bit to make it a less potent weapon. But not taking its authority seriously is precisely the problem. Those wielding it as a weapon are not submitting to it. They're yelling through its disjointed pieces, as opposed to expressing the whole. They close tight around some point they take a fancy to, instead of opening up to the Voice that pierces to the marrow. Authority is not the problem. Closed allegiance is the problem.

The authority of the Word is primarily creative; after all. The entire created order in all its variety came about through "the word of God." In Christ's parable of the four soils, the Word planted in receptive hearts is capable of bearing fruit a hundredfold. When Paul was cut off from his field of work in a Roman dungeon he took comfort in the fact that "the word of God is not imprisoned." It was still out there in Asia Minor where he had left it, performing feats and overcoming adversaries. It still created new life, though the apostle's was coming to an end.

That's another reason Scripture can inspire open allegiance; it's the creative Word of God within which people grow and expand. Open allegiance keeps making discoveries in the riches of the Word; it keeps seeking to change. Closed allegiance, on the other hand, tends to see the Word as information to conquer. You finalize on the truth you see in it and then proceed to dig in and defend your position.

Open allegiance does see absolute truths in Scripture, but it also sees the challenge of applying them, expanding on them, expressing them in new ways. The Word must be continually spoken, its essential form continually fleshed out. The Word must continually come to life.

Chapter Fifteen

THE EPIC OF OPEN ALLEGIANCE

Scripture itself provides its own illuminating epic about open allegiance to the truth and making a meaningful statement in the world. Different characters all through the Bible highlight the importance of this virtue—both through their failures and their successes.

Fumbling the Truth

The patriarchs as a whole had a hard time making a stand in the wilds of Canaan. Though caught up in the adventure of following after the God of Heaven, they were still basically adolescents in the faith and often wandered off course.

Abram choked while waiting out a famine in Egypt. He was sure his hosts would kill him to get his beautiful wife Sarah. So he asked her to say she was his sister. Maybe he could protect her better that way, Abram rationalized. The rookie patriarch was not yet ready to take a stand on truth and let God take care of the consequences.

Pharoah did take a fancy to Sarah, but when he found out Abram had deceived him, he was deeply offended and sent the whole clan packing. Abram's cowardice brought reproach on the name of his God.

God gave him a new name: Abraham. But he choked again while

staying in Gerar with King Abimelech. Abraham told him the same lie about Sarah being his sister. The patriarch still couldn't stand with both feet on the truth. Abimelech brought Sarah into his harem and God had to intervene, warning the king in a dream. Abraham once more slinked off from a near-disaster.

His son Isaac took up the habit. He told Philistine neighbors that his beautiful wife Rebekah was his sister, afraid they might kill him to get to her. But those neighbors proved more upright than he. When the Philistine king found out Rebekah was Isaac's wife, he ordered that no one touch the woman on pain of death.

The next generation fell into the same mishandling of the truth. When Isaac was almost blind and about to die, his son Jacob impersonated brother Esau in order to steal the birthright blessing. After the deception unraveled, the family fell apart.

Taking a stand on the truth under pressure did not come easy to the founders of God's holy nation. But one man finally did, with wonderful results. Betrayed by his own brothers, sold as a slave, separated from his beloved father, isolated in an alien culture, a youthful Joseph made a courageous stand. He refused to take the easy way up the ladder by sleeping with the boss's amorous wife. Wrong was still wrong even in a world where no one had heard of Yahweh.

Joseph stood upright even in a dungeon. That's where his refusal of the woman's advances landed him. He helped others cheerfully. When the chance finally came to get out of jail and into power on the strength of his prophetic gift, Joseph still stood with both feet on the truth. He made plain to Pharoah that it wasn't his own store of knowledge that enabled him to interpret the monarch's dream and see the future. It was a revelation from the God who sees all and knows all. Joseph's allegiance to God produced great results during a terrible famine. His foresight saved thousands from starvation—including his own clan. Yahweh's name was honored before the heathen.

A Courageous Few

During subsequent centuries, Israel carved out a place for itself in Canaan, became a monarchy, prospered, divided, was reformed, and then decayed. In this period, one conflict dominates the story: the struggle against idolatry. The truth about a God who rules over all faced a constant challenge from other deities. These idols pictured only pieces of God that could be manipulated according to what you needed.

Fertility cults majored in sex, violence, local protection, and good crops. They proved to be strong competition for the God of atonement symbols and ten commandments. Prophets came on the scene to campaign on behalf of the truth, the whole truth and nothing but the truth. Their "Thus sayeth the Lord," called out to a people constantly tripped up by altars to Baal.

In the third year of his reign, godly King Jehoshaphat of Judah ventured north on a visit to morally dangerous ground: the palace of Israel's King Ahab. Ahab had "sold himself to do evil in the eyes of the Lord, urged on by Jezebel his wife." But more recently, in response to the gruesome death of the evil queen and some pointed words from the prophet Elijah, he'd humbled himself before God in sackcloth and earned a temporary reprieve. Jehoshaphat probably wanted to see if Ahab had really been converted.

As the two kings talked, Ahab brought up the subject of Ramoth Gilead, an Israelite city that had been taken by the king of Aram. He proposed that the two join forces and recapture the town. Jehoshaphat declared himself and his forces at Ahab's service, but suggested that they first "seek counsel of the Lord."

Ahab happened to have four hundred in-house prophets to call on. They were ushered in and asked, "Shall I go to war against Ramoth Gilead, or shall I refrain?"

The men responded unanimously: "Go for the Lord will give it into the king's hand."

Jehoshaphat was a bit suspicious of these eager faces dishing out the truth so quickly. How had Ahab, a recent convert from years of Baal worship, managed to surround himself with so many spokesmen for God? They all looked over-programmed. So he asked, "Is there not a prophet of the Lord here whom we can inquire of?"

Ahab groaned and replied that there was one man who claimed the right credentials, but he had a very negative attitude. Micaiah son of Imlah had never said one good thing about him.

Jehoshaphat thought the man should be summoned anyway and Ahab consented. While Micaiah was on his way, the 400 hired voices tried to be more convincing and worked themselves into a frenzy of positive reinforcement. "Attack Ramoth Gilead and be victorious," they shouted. One put on a pair of iron horns, danced around, and declared, "With these you will gore the Arameans until they are destroyed."

Meanwhile, the messenger sent to fetch God's prophet gave Micaiah a pointed word of advice: "Look, as one man the other prophets are predicting success for the king. Let your word agree with theirs, and speak favorably."

But Micaiah would not agree that truth can be established by acclamation. He looked the messenger square in the eye and said, "I can only tell him what the Lord tells me."

The two arrived on the scene and Micaiah stood before the monarchs in their royal robes, surrounded by a 400-prophet-strong message. Ahab turned wearily him and asked, "Micaiah, shall we go to war . . . or shall I refrain?"

The other voices quieted. Ahab stared angrily. After testing him a bit, to see if he really wanted to know, Micaiah gave it to Ahab with both barrels: "I saw all Israel scattered on the hills like sheep without a shepherd."[1]

Ahab's resolve to hear the truth collapsed. He turned to Jehoshaphat with a didn't-I-tell-you-so look and complained: there was that negative attitude again.

But Micaiah kept going. He stood before the hundreds of disapproving prophets and told Ahab that they had become lying spirits leading him toward disaster. Their head man slapped Micaiah, but he stood firm. In the end, Ahab sent God's prophet off to prison and stubbornly marched off to the predicted disaster.

Prophets stood against the tide, and some kings even listened. The bright spots in Israel's history—Asa, Jehoshaphat, Joash, Hezekiah, Josiah—took stands on the basis of God's truth, the Word, the covenant, and tried to turn back the tide.

Josiah is a particularly illuminating example. Arriving on the scene when Judah was deep into its decline, he decided to have Jerusalem's neglected temple repaired. While cleaning up the premises, a priest named Hilkiah discovered the "Book of the Law of the Lord." It contained the old covenant, the moral transaction between Jehovah and His people that created this unique entity called Israel.

Josiah had a scribe read the book to him; he listened to God's expectations for his people spelled out and heard the litany of blessings and cursings that finalized the covenant. And the Word hit home.

Its authority had not changed. Josiah felt anguish over the awful distance his people had come from their noble origins. He felt the hot breath of judgment hovering over them. The king ripped his royal robes apart and wept as one who mourns a death.

Josiah took a stand. He initiated reforms, removed idols, re-instituted the Passover and personally lead the citizens of Jerusalem to make a commitment to "perform the words of the covenant written in this book."

Tragedy and Triumph

For the prophet Jeremiah, the Word was something he found and consumed. It became "a joy and the delight of my heart." But the Word was also a fire burning in his belly that would not let him rest. It was a strain holding it in; Jeremiah had to speak or die, and when he did speak he made the loneliest, most courageous stand in the Old Testament. Jeremiah told his people they were resolutely heading toward oblivion. He proclaimed that iniquity is a stain which can't be brushed away. Jeremiah grew more unpopular with each livid oracle he delivered. Corrupt priests and gutless kings tried to silence him on several occasions. But nothing could compromise the truth that propelled this man against the tide.

Jeremiah's irrepressible moral voice and Judah's decadence came to a head during Nebuchadnezzar's seige of Jerusalem when his forces threatened the city with destruction. Those prophets-for-hire were still mouthing their cheap good news: God will surely rescue His people and destroy Babylon. But Jeremiah had to lay out the cold truth from his Lord: "See, I am setting before you the way of life and the way of death. Whoever stays in this city will die by the sword, famine, or plague. But whoever goes out and surrenders to the Babylonians who are besieging you will live; he will escape with his life."[2]

To the Jews, the chosen people of God, those could only be the words of a traitor. Jeremiah must be palming shekels from Nebuchadnezzar. A prophet of Jehovah urging abandonment of the Holy City? Impossible.

Persecution intensified. But Jeremiah could not change the message. He even predicted that the temple would be as thoroughly destroyed as Israel's desolate Shiloh. The sanctity of the building could not somehow excuse the willful lack of holiness among those wor-

142

shiping in it. This outraged the priests. Their temple was sacred, period, no matter what corruption might slip into its courts. To surrender it to heathen hands seemed sheer blasphemy.

Jeremiah was threatened, imprisoned, thrown into a cistern, mocked, and treated as a traitor. But that didn't change his allegiance to the facts; the fire burned on. This prophet shows us not only great courage in his single-handed campaign for the truth, but also the terrible anguish of a sensitive man who is misunderstood and isolated. There is nothing glamorous about his stand. It was a terribly difficult position to take. But the truth gave him no alternative. Jeremiah kept pleading to the end.

If he shows us open allegiance within a tragedy, a prophet named Daniel gives us a more hopeful picture. He took a courageous stand with three Hebrew friends in the courts of the conquerer, Nebuchadnezzar. It started with the food at the king's table, which he was to partake of as one of those in training for the king's personal service. Daniel didn't whine apologetically that he had to follow certain dietary rules peculiar to his religion. He offered to demonstrate that God's way was best; it would stand up to the test. Daniel proposed the first comparative dietary study, and he and his three friends came out looking healthier after ten days.

This faithfulness in the details of their religion led to faithfulness when the big test came—out on the plain of Dura with thousands of emissaries from around the empire bowing down on cue to the statue of gold which Nebuchadnezzar had erected. Daniel's friends, Shadrach, Meshach, and Abednego, could not agree with the majority. This personification of Babylon lifted high above them was not the kingdom they were looking forward to. It was not the rock that would become a holy mountain and fill up the whole world. They could not bow down.

Nebuchadnezzar's firm words of advice didn't move them. The sight of blazing furnaces waiting to receive the irreverent didn't move them. Not even the flames up close and personal shook their resolve to keep standing when everyone else bowed to the lie.

And this time tragedy gave way to a glorious deliverance. The three Hebrew youths stood upright and unharmed in the furnace, just as they had before the statue of gold. God came very close.

The Most Eloquent Stand

The Old Testament story of Israel stumbling over and over before idols manages to end on this triumphant note of three men ram-rod straight no matter what the consequences. And it flows into God's great stand in Galilee. The long line of men and women expressing allegiance to the Word against the tide comes to a climax in the Word Himself standing among us.

Jesus made the Word tangible as its perfect embodiment. He magnified the law as a basis for artful goodness and contrasted it with stifling human traditions. He confronted a very closed type of allegiance and emphasized a religion of excelling in the Spirit.

What's the law all about? Loving God with all your being and your neighbor as yourself. No intricate ethical dilemmas here; the emphasis is on values that can take you a long way above the law. He understood primary principles, and he exposed whatever contradicted those principles.

Jesus condensed the Word to its essentials: love God with all your heart and mind; love your neighbor as yourself. He also expanded those essentials to something bigger and greater than the religious tradition around him could encompass. The Word had been withered into a multiplicity of petty details. Jesus brought it back to its original vitality.

Love as an abstraction became the healing of lepers, care for the poor, a welcome for outcasts, deliverance from demons. The Word did things that no one had ever seen before. A man born blind received his sight. Lazarus exited his own tomb, hale and hearty.

The temple in Jerusalem stood for something as a house of prayer. But merchants and money-changers had made it into a lie. The truth about God welcoming sinners who come for mercy had been terribly distorted. So here Jesus acted most directly and violently against evil. Using His own bare hands, He made the temple speak once again with an authentic voice. The exploiters fled and the needy returned, led by children's praises.

Jesus spelled out His open allegiance to the Word—all the while spied upon, interrogated, harassed, and criticized by His rivals, by a tradition that had proclaimed squatter's rights over the truth. Finally Christ's enemies would test His allegiance to the limit on Golgotha by means of the horrors of crucifixion. But there He made the most important statement of all time. On the cross He welcomed all comers into the living Word until the end, creating a place where the weakest and most misguided can stand securely and become strong.

Chapter Sixteen

A WITHERED HAND
IN THE SYNAGOGUE

The narrative of patriarch and prophet leaning hard on a truth bigger than themselves leads us into New Testament teaching. That's where this matter of declaring our allegiance by taking a stand is nailed down. Paul declared: "We can do nothing against the truth, but only for the truth."[1] His statement expresses a confidence that God's reality will ultimately prevail. It also expresses a resolve never to betray that truth. Believers are urged to cling to the word, loyally confess the faith, and be faithful until death. We are to stand fast in the "true grace of God," "stand firm and hold to the teachings," "stand firm in all the will of God," "stand firm in the faith," "stand firm in the Lord." Paul wrote the Thessalonians that their valor meant everything to him: "For now we really live, since you are standing firm in the Lord."[2]

Taking a stand matters; but this allegiance is not an end in itself; the place where we stand is what gives it value. We stand in God, in His will, teachings, and grace. It's His revelation of Himself that gives us a meaningful statement to make in the world. We find a truth that will stay put, and so we are enabled to stay put.

Gold Versus Straw

In the epistles, we also begin to see the essential components of open allegiance. We get a clearer picture of how it works, what it produces.

First, when we stand on the whole of God's Word, when we remain open to its Big Picture, we automatically avoid standing in a lot of foolish places. Just as with light humility and hard honor, open allegiance clears away a lot of life's clutter. If we emphasize what the Word emphasizes, if we are passionate about what it is passionate about, then we won't get sidetracked; we won't make big stands on little issues. There are a great many noisy battles that turn out to be mostly smoke when examined with a good dose of the Word; a great many battlegrounds turn into mirages.

Those who maintain an open allegiance must be diligent workmen "handling accurately the word of truth." [3] The Word is not a blunt instrument that we may grab most anywhere and use to pound against "error." It is a finely crafted tool which, when used correctly, pierces to the marrow.

The Word is powerful because it helps us get to the heart of things. Its principles are surgically precise. Everything is laid bare before it. The benign is separated from the malignant. The Word shows us what is vital; what's worth taking a stand on.

The scribes and Pharisees gathered on a certain Sabbath day in a Galilean synagogue kept glancing from the rabbi commenting on Scripture to a man with a withered hand seated in front. They were hoping that the itinerant teacher, Jesus of Nazareth, would incriminate Himself before the Law. They were hoping He'd do it right there as He, draped in customary prayer shawl, was attempting to explain the Word to them.

These men had caught Jesus' disciples in a transgression on the previous Sabbath. The twelve had been passing through a grain field and, being hungry, plucked some stalks, rubbed the heads of wheat in their palms and ate the grain. Technically, this could be considered harvesting and thus an act of labor on the Sabbath. When the spying scribes objected, Jesus had replied, "The Sabbath was made for man, not man for the Sabbath." [4]

That didn't seem at all like an explanation and they determined to nail this rival teacher as a Sabbath breaker. So they made sure that a prime candidate for healing was seated prominently in the synagogue as Jesus spoke. Healing, in their minds, was also labor, and thus prohibited on the Sabbath.

After rolling up the scroll and placing it in its place, Jesus, sure enough, looked at the man with a shriveled hand and asked him to come and stand in front of everyone. And then He hurled His challenge at the heart of the legalistic religion that was choking the life out of His people. He stared at the Pharisees and asked angrily, "Which is lawful on the Sabbath: to do good or to do evil, to save life or to kill?" [4]

Jesus' adversaries couldn't reply; they were not prepared to deal with big principles, only to defend the petty rules they'd built around their religious turf. Jesus seemed to be reading their thoughts. They were plotting about how to eliminate this charismatic rival—and here He was about to save life from decay. "To save life or to kill?" For a moment they felt nailed to the wall. When Jesus asked the man to stretch out his arm, and then restored it to wholeness, they could say nothing in rebuttal to the awed congregation.

Jesus took a stand by healing people on the Sabbath. Those acts spotlighted a religion of compassion and rebuked a religion of petty legalism. They demonstrated that the whole complicated structure of regulations guarded by the Jewish elite wasn't that important. Those rules often stood in opposition to basic human and divine values. Jesus' simple acts of mercy swept that clutter away. He swept it away as if it were a pile of bones in a whitewashed sepulcher. Jesus' stand embodied a vital principle: the priority of loving people. That's more important than religious conventions.

Open allegiance to the Word highlights what matters more. It calls for a degree of discernment. Our eyes need to be trained to find that hidden treasure and that pearl of great price in the rough. By continual exposure to the "solid food" of the Word, those aiming for open allegiance "have trained themselves to distinguish good from evil." [6] They concentrate on a "sincere and pure devotion to Christ." [7] By not allowing themselves to be led astray from the primary values of Scripture, they tell the difference between doctrinal edifices built of gold, silver, and precious stones, and those made of wood, hay and straw.

How to Stand

Paul took a definite stand in the first century. He championed the gospel of grace against all comers, giving a precise, theological shape to the revolution that Jesus had begun. There were quite a few people around the early believers who would have gutted the gospel. They wanted to keep certain Jewish traditions as a kind of security blanket. Circumcision, holy days, and ceremonies assured them they were the chosen. Paul consistently rejected these external symbols of the old covenant, not because they were immoral, but because they were pointing people to the wrong kind of assurance. The atonement of Christ had to remain at the center. If that foundation stone of salvation by grace through faith were discarded, then that enslaving system of legalism that Jesus had overturned would fall on them again.

So Paul fought and fought very hard. He opposed certain Galatians who were trying to insert circumcision and the law between believers and grace. He opposed Colossians who were trying to insert asceticism between believers and grace. He opposed individuals in Rome who were under the illusion that possessing the Law meant they would be justified by it instead of by faith alone. Paul cried out for a pure gospel. As a result he gave Christians down through the ages a solid and safe defense from the chronic plague of legalism. His was a very courageous stand. The apostle generally had to make his points on the run; always some fanatical group had pledged to do away with him.

But here's the most remarkable thing about Paul's stand: it was based on open allegiance. This is something all too rare in our world. Most people who are compelled to take a strong stand against "error" end up with a closed allegiance. They don't grow. They are wielding the truth so tightly that it can't expand in their hands. Human beings have a hard time standing firm on important principles and yet remaining flexible about lesser ones.

But Paul, that former Pharisee of Pharisees, shows us how to take a stand and still retain an open allegiance. Notice, for example, how he dealt with the issue of food offered to idols. Some of the meat sold in the marketplaces of the ancient world had been offered to idols. Christians wondered whether it was OK to purchase it. Was the meat somehow defiled or even dangerous because it had been placed on altars to Athena or Jupiter? To those who had just come out of a pagan world, the meat shouted idol worship. To other believers it was just food.

Paul was asked his advice. You might expect this champion of a pure gospel to flail against any form of "compromise." Instead, he exhibited a sensitive regard for the feelings of those concerned. He believed that pagan gods held no power over the worshipers of Jesus Christ. Food offered to them had no magical power to harm. But he also recognized that, "Some people are still so accustomed to idols that when they eat such food they think of it as having been sacrificed to an idol, and since their conscience is weak, it is defiled."[8] Fear of this food offered to idols was a kind of weakness, a lack of maturity and of confidence in the gospel of grace. But it was not an evil to oppose. Paul advised: "Accept him whose faith is weak, without passing judgment on disputable matters."[9]

Above all the apostle wanted empathy in matters where a person's subjective reaction was what made something healthy or unhealthy. "The man who eats everything must not look down on him who does not, and the man who does not eat everything must not condemn the man who does, for God has accepted him."[10] Paul warned those who felt free to eat the sacrificed meat not to become a "stumbling block" to their more sensitive brothers, saying, in effect: my eating it can be perfectly fine for me, but if it's harmful for my brother, I'll avoid it out of courtesy.

Paul fought hard for the cause of Christian freedom, but he dealt very gently with those who hadn't yet let go of all their security blankets. When questioned about which Jewish traditions involving ceremonial foods and holy days one might still observe as a believer in the Messiah, Paul counseled: "Each man should be fully convinced in his own mind."[11]

Here he seems totally opposite from the man waging war against "Judaisers," the man who opposed any compromise to the pure gospel as evil. The difference is this: his battle cries were directed against men deliberately attempting to subvert the gospel, wolves in sheep's clothing who were seeking power in a congregation by imposing their own brand of legalism. They posed a clear and present danger to the gospel of grace that was just beginning to bear fruit. These men were not working out the problem of new wineskins for new wine. They were poisoning the new wine itself. They simply would not accept the cornerstone of justification by faith. This was a wrong to oppose, and Paul gave his life proclaiming an opposite allegiance.

On the other hand, his words of understanding were directed toward people who *were* struggling to work out the problem of new wineskins: what new religious practices might best express the new gospel of grace. Some were barely fumbling toward a faith in Christ's atonement. But Paul accepted that. He saw that this was not compromise, but growth. He encouraged that growth—gently and skillfully "like a mother caring for her little children." [12]

Paul shows us how to stand, how to oppose evil. So many times we fight the wrong battles in the church; we pound on splinters as if they were the crossbeams of truth. We erect a superstructure around a few doctrinal gargoyles on the roof while the foundation of love, grace and peace decays underneath us.

Paul opposed evil, real evil. But he could also nurture the weak. His firm stand was based on a truth central in the life and death of Christ. He firmly opposed individuals with selfish motives who deliberately undermined that truth.

There are times when we need to be flexible. There are times when we need to listen instead of speaking. They are times when we need to seek God's guidance about whether some "error" we're opposing might not be a new truth that's hitting our blind spot.

There are also times when we have to meet evil head-on. There are times when the moral authority of Scripture asks us to go into battle. "Put on the full armor of God, so that when the day of evil comes, you may be able to stand your ground." [13] Some have been moved by the Word to make strategic protests that have changed history.

Energy from the Word

William Wilberforce's powerful oratory won him election to parliament from Yorkshire in 1780. His prominent family and quick wit won him a welcome into London's elegant private clubs and scandalous parties. He was speeding on toward upper-class privileges and political advancement. But then an old schoolmaster interrupted. They were vacationing through the Swiss Alps together, debating the fine points of politics in their carriage, when the subject of religion came up. Wilberforce treated it flippantly at first, but the schoolmaster kept talking in earnest. At length, Wilberforce agreed to begin reading the Scriptures daily.

The Word took hold. In the midst of parliament's summer session and the whirl of London social life, Wilberforce couldn't help seeing things differently. He began to notice the corruption and oppression around him. Continuing with his study of the Bible, Wilberforce was led to commit his life to Jesus Christ.

His new perspective deepened as he started each day with a time of prayer and Bible reading. One morning, he read a clergyman's impassioned account of the horrors of the slave trade and found his life calling. Wilberforce's open allegiance to the truth compelled him to take a stand. He began speaking out in parliament against a very profitable tide that was enriching the British Empire. He began pouring out his powerful oratory on behalf of the black men, woman, and children who were bleeding, starving, and suffocating to death in the holds of British ships.

The opposition marshaled its forces. Africans are happy to escape the barbarities of their homeland, they assured the country. Two-thirds of England's commerce would disappear if the slave trade were abolished, they warned.

For a time the claims of business drowned out Wilberforce's pleas for justice. But this sickly, diminutive orator would not stop. A small group gathered around him, men devoted to Christ and the abolition of the slave trade. They distributed thousands of pamphlets, spoke at public meetings, circulated petitions and organized a boycott of slave-grown sugar.

They brought the slave question up for a vote year after year in parliament, never giving in to defeat. At one especially low point, Wilberforce opened his Bible and out fell a letter, written to him years before from John Wesley. It read in part, "Unless God has raised you up for this very thing, you will be worn out by the opposition of men and devils, but if God be for you who can be against you?"

Finally, after years of frustration, a bill banning the slave trade passed, February 4, 1807 at 4:00 A.M. Shortly afterward, Wilberforce and his friends burst from their chambers out into the dark, snow-covered street and celebrated like schoolboys, running around, clapping each other on the back, shouting their joy. When the group gathered for a quieter celebration at Wilberforce's house, he turned to a friend who'd worked with him through the years of struggle, illness, ridicule and defeat, and said with a twinkle in his eyes, "Well, Henry, what do we abolish next?"[14]

William Wilberforce could never have waged that lonely struggle without the momentum of Scripture behind him. He certainly could never have emerged from that long battle with a light in his eyes.

Christ's Word had sustained him. It wasn't some isolated text that Wilberforce stood on. The opposition had its share of isolated texts. He was sustained by the whole thrust of Scripture. He absorbed the Old Testament prophets calling for justice on behalf of the oppressed and the New Testament proclamation that every individual is claimed by Christ. To this Wilberforce gave his wholehearted allegiance. His daily reading, his familiarity with the spirit of Scripture as well as its clear commands, gave him the energy to stand so eloquently for its principles.

Proving What's Best

Open allegiance opposes evil, but it also does more: it demonstrates that God's way is best. This is another essential component. "All Scripture is God-breathed and is useful for teaching, rebuking, correcting and training in righteousness. . . ."[15] The Bible enlightens as well as confronts. Those who take a stand with it can teach as well as rebuke, show as well as tell. It's not enough to complain about fallen standards, we need to present the values of the Word in place of what is wrong.

Open allegiance requires a feisty faith in the ability of the eternal, the unseen, to out-perform the things that are temporary. Those whose minds are renewed by the Word are eager to "prove what the will of God is, that which is good and acceptable and perfect."[16] They believe that the "good fight of faith" can demonstrate an eternal quality of life in the world. They believe that it is possible to "do it all for the glory of God," demonstrating that His way is best.

This is how our religion expands. This is how it becomes something big and compelling for our contemporaries. Here's where our allegiance must become the most creative. Some believers have actually fashioned clever experiments in which the Word can demonstrate its truthfulness.

When Hudson Taylor went to China, he had a special burden for those who had never heard about Christ. So he traveled far inland where Europeans ventured only at the risk of their lives. He sailed up remote rivers, visiting village after village as a healer and teacher. Taylor managed to survive unscathed and also attract others to his quest.

In 1876, after ten years of labor, more than seventy people had devoted their lives to spreading the gospel in the vast hinterland of the Middle Kingdom. Financial support for the China Inland Mission had never failed; it had never been in debt. And it had all happened without making any kind of appeal for funds.

Taylor believed that God's promises were something to stake a claim on. They must find expression in real life. He had decided that he would depend on God alone to finance his mission to China. No begging, no appeal letters, no hinting about needs. If all those statements in Scripture about God's faithfulness and watch-care were true, why not demonstrate it—in the remotest corner of the world.

At the beginning of 1887, Taylor realized that still more millions in China waited to hear the Word. So he and his fellow workers asked God for what seemed like the impossible: one hundred new volunteers that year and £10,000 of additional income to support them. The year ended after a great deal of prayer, but no appeals for money, with the last of "The Hundred" on their way to China and £11,000 of extra income.

Taylor wanted the entire project based on the biblical assurance, "Jehovah Jireh"—*God provides*. Everyone had to accept the experiment: go to God directly to take care of needs, rely entirely on His benevolent will.

Taylor was not reluctant to talk about the need for missionaries. He published a periodical called "China's Millions" in order to arouse complacent Christians. He acknowledged gifts received in the magazine and, of course, the mission attracted its regular supporters.

But Taylor wanted God in direct control. He would never plead for money. He sometimes spoke at Christian conferences while recruiting missionaries back in England. More than once someone would rise to take up a collection after one of his stirring messages. But Taylor always stopped it; he did not want money coming in because of his eloquence and above all he did not want to divert funds from other church missions. If the Lord wanted a certain project to go forward He Himself would have to direct people to supply the funds.

Time after time Taylor and his friends tested the authoritative Word and found it dependable in meeting specific needs. Once while traveling by train from a conference back to London, Hudson met a certain Count Bobrinksy. The Russian nobleman had heard of the China Inland Mission and, taking out his pocketbook, said: "Let me give you a trifle toward your work."

Taylor glanced at the bank note handed to him and thought there'd been some mistake. "Did you not mean to give me five pounds?" he said quickly. "Please let me return this note; it is for fifty."

The Count was a bit surprised too, but reflecting a moment he replied, "I cannot take it back. It was five pounds I meant to give, but God must have intended you to have fifty; I cannot take it back."

When Taylor arrived at the mission headquarters on Pyrland Road, he found a prayer meeting in progress. The workers there were about to send a remittance out to China, but the money on hand was 49 pounds, 11 shillings short. As usual they didn't accept the deficiency as inevitable but had made it a matter of prayer—going to the Source and His unfailing promises. When Taylor laid the bank note he'd just received on the table it did seem to have come directly from a Heavenly Father's hand. [17]

Hudson Taylor took a stand out in China. He wanted to make a statement to complacent Christians. Most of his contemporaries might give lip service to God as the Provider. But they would never think of actually depending on him. Taylor demonstrated there was a better way. However he didn't harangue Victorian England about its pathetic lack of genuine faith; he didn't rebuke Christians for not putting their money where their mouth was. He simply showed that God had a better way.

There are times when we have to fight an evil like slavery head-on. Explicit Scripture passages about justice impel us to go into battle. But other matters require that we express our allegiance in a different way. Asking for money is not an evil. Scripture does not prescribe fund-raising methods; it simply encourages generosity.

But Hudson Taylor wanted to flesh out an important principle. The Bible encourages people to trust God implicitly about everything. He wanted to demonstrate that trust. He wanted to show that it worked in the real world. And this missionary managed to isolate God's gracious provisions on a canvas in remotest China. It's an impressive composition. God the Provider stands brightly lit; every bit of extraneous scenery is cut away. This is a beautiful piece of artful goodness. Our faith is enlarged because of it.

A Place for Others

Demonstrating an open allegiance to God's Word can sweep away the trivial, spotlight important truths, oppose real evil, and demonstrate that God's way is best. It can also create room for other people to stand.

Hebrews describes heroes of the faith as a great cloud of witnesses who cheer on those coming after them. They inspire us to persevere. Standing in faith against the tide they had to keep an eye on a better country, a heavenly one, where the truth they sacrificed for would find fulfillment. They welcomed that promise from a distance. The world was not worthy of them, but their allegiance creates a legacy on earth that nurtures moral courage. These are people who help create a place for us to stand.

As rows of subdued waves stroked the Guam shoreline, a crescent of palms nodded off to sleep in the breeze. Two men squatting on a gnarled piece of driftwood gazed out at dusk settling over the bay.

Captain Graff's voice was calm now, even kind: "Mosley, we've got a big job to do over here; it's going to take all we've got."

"Yes, sir." Chief Yeoman Ramon Mosley was even quieter.

"We're not out on some Sunday school picnic. This is war. The Navy has got to maintain complete discipline."

"Yes, sir."

"Mosley," the captain sounded like a long-suffering parent, "You know what I'm going to have to do don't you?"

The chief yeoman looked down at the moist sand and replied, "Yes, Cap'n. What you've got to do, I guess you've just got to do."

Captain Graff slowly stood up, spat into the sea, and ambled back to the line of forest green tents.

Mosley knew very well what his commanding officer had to do. That unnerving fact had been pressed down on him for quite some time. Anyone refusing duty in battle conditions was subject to execution. It was hard for Mosley to imagine getting shot by his own countrymen, and yet slowly, persistently, the formal confrontations were leading to that point.

The monotonous gray of the sea stretched out before him like some unintelligible scroll. Somewhere on the other side Frances wrote letters. He would get them only in fragments. As a sailor under arrest, confined to the base, even his incoming mail was censored.

That other world where people loved, tended farms, and had children was becoming more and more intangible. He felt like an odd speck drifting in a world turned upside down.

Maybe they were right. Maybe he *was* crazy. Maybe he *was* the only one holding such bizarre opinions.

And yet how could he forget those wonderful moments God's Word became so clear and present? He and Frances had been newlyweds in New Orleans. They joined a Bible Study in their apartment building led by a Seventh-day Adventist pastor. He opened up truths they had never seen before. Ramon and Frances learned about exciting themes that emerged from the whole of the Bible. They saw the big picture, from Eden lost to Eden regained, fall into place.

One of the truths they discovered was the Sabbath God instituted as a memorial of Creation. The couple often prayed at dusk on the roof of their building. Looking out over New Orleans, they had talked about their growing conviction that they should keep the Sabbath truly as the Lord's Day. They began to believe that the commandment to do no work on this day and set it apart as holy time, was God's will for Christians.

The test had not come at first, not until their convictions had solidified and the couple had slipped in too deep to get out. For a while, out on shore patrol in the Gulf with the Navy, Mosley had been able to arrange for weekly time off. But finally the immovable object dropped in front of him: a direct order to work on Sabbath.

Mosley painfully remembered the letters to Washington asking for hospital duty, refusals, changes of status, verbal blasts from an assortment of officers. It all lead to one ingenious solution: "Well, Mosley, we're going to see what you do on your Sabbath when the Japs get after you."

The incorrigible sailor was put on a transfer to the Solomon Islands and assigned to a Higgins landing craft unit. Surely one good landing amid machine gun fire would cure him of his scruples.

Mosley sailed out of New Orleans on a huge transport ship. Leaning over the steel deck rail into the salty raw gusts of the night, he knew exactly why he was being shipped out. He'd taken a stand. But there was no warm feeling welling up inside, no cymbals crashing. He felt only the cold wedge of conscience with which he'd tried to fend off their attacks: "If you operate on what you think is right, you just can't take any other stand."

Mosley had made chief yeoman on board ship and, as chief petty officer, was placed in charge of the personnel office on Guam after the marines established a beachhead.

Technically on a seven-day work week, he had managed to quietly arrange for time off during the Sabbath. But one day the commanding officer walked into his tent and found him studying his Sabbath School lesson. The trouble began all over again.

Now as the sky blackened overhead, Mosley knew he would be facing increasing pressures to give in. But he also knew that the cold wedge was still in place. Mosley stood up, spit into the sea and strolled back to his quarters.

The next day a summons came from Captain Graff's tent. Mosley walked in and saluted. He knew what was coming, another "session." Graff, several executive officers, marshals and the chaplain sat in full-dress uniform in a row around him. Their clustered brass displayed the authority which Mosley had been drilled to obey without question.

"You have a duty to your country."

"Men are being killed all around you."

"How come you're so sure you're the only one who's right?"

Each one in turn whipped out a biting monologue, threatening, pleading, shaming this man they could not fathom.

After an hour the chief yeoman's face began betraying his weariness and confusion. He couldn't answer all their accusations. Then Captain Graff struck a final swift blow: "Mosley, in this situation you have no choice. You cannot disobey a direct order. You will work seven days as scheduled."

Out of his haze the lone sailor managed to reply, "Sir, I have to do the only thing left for me to do. It is impossible for me to carry out . . ." He did not finish.

Graff blew up. "You WILL work Mosley. Medals and insignia shook on the captain's chest. "If you think you can defy this whole command you're in for a big surprise sailor." Graff continued with an assortment of ear-burning curses before thundering, "DISMISSED."

When "deck court" finally arrived, it was almost a relief. At least the sessions would end. Mosley had at first been docketed for a court martial. But an Adventist physician, a full Commander on a Navy ship, wrote a letter to Admiral Nimitz on his behalf. He pointed out that the right of people to worship as their conscience dictated was one of the things the Navy was defending in the Pacific. Probably as a result of that letter, Mosley faced a less punitive deck court.

Beside two flags and three stiff marshals, Captain Graff read the charges and his prepared verdict. Mosley was reduced to first-class yeoman, reprimanded for insubordination, and stripped of his duties in the personnel office.

The captain then ordered him out to a rusting, decrepit barge that accommodated a few cubbyhole offices. Confined to the base, Mosley spent months in uneasy limbo, trying hard to find work that would keep him from further confrontations. But he felt grateful to have survived and not betrayed his Lord.

Legacy

One day an ambulance pulled up near the old barges. A young man with lieutenant bars stepped out and began asking for a guy named Mosley. Everybody knew about Mosley. The yeoman was quickly brought out. He saluted and identified himself.

The lieutenant extended his hand. "Glad to meet you. I'm a Seventh-day Adventist too."

Mosley stood there for a moment stunned. He felt like a man long wandering in the desert who catches the scent of water. So there *was* another one in the world, right here in front of him. So he *wasn't* all crazy. Suddenly tears burned in Mosley's eyes. He struggled for something to say to keep the mirage from disappearing. "How did you find out . . . I mean. . . ."

"Well, our hospital ship landed on the other side last week, and I heard about this odd guy who was having trouble over his religion."

"I haven't been able to locate another Adventist since I left the States."

"Hey, well, listen—there are some more of us on the ship. And we're thinking of trying to start some sort of church service here."

"Sounds great."

"I think we've got some of the Guamanians interested too. We really think this is a providential opportunity. This may be our only chance to start a church on the island."

After they retired to Mosley's tiny office, the lieutenant explained that Guam had been dominated by a powerful bishop who would permit no other religious mission to enter the island. When the Japanese took Guam, they captured the bishop and sent him to the Philippines. So if they moved fast they might be able to get something going.

"There's only one problem," the lieutenant said, "we need a place to meet."

It would always remain a complete mystery to Mosley how he managed to walk into the office of the commanding officer he had last seen at deck court. But there he was with his request, saluting a stone-faced captain Graff. "Captain," he began, "We have some Christian sailors in a hospital company here who'd like to meet together and we need some kind of place to worship in."

The commanding officer looked down at his desk and began writing. Mosley decided to go on. "I saw this old storage tent, sir, down by D barracks that nobody is using. I wonder if we could perhaps borrow it."

Suddenly Graff stood up and stared into the yeoman's eyes. "Listen, Mosley," he said, pointing his finger, "You don't have to use that thing. Let me get you a good tent." The captain marched out of his office and led his awed subordinate over to a corrugated tin warehouse. There he ordered the supply officer to get Mosley a good tent, "just the size he wants."

Next, Graff took Mosley over to the Lutheran chaplain. "This man is going to start a worship service. Fix him up with whatever he needs," Graff commanded. Quickly, Mosley's arms were filled with gold and silver bowls, cups and crucifixes. Being in no position to refuse the weighty gesture, he thanked the chaplain and left.

Graff wasn't finished. "Now, Mosley, let's see, you're going to need something to transport this stuff. Let me arrange for a truck and driver." A truck was requisitioned and loaded. Mosley hurried off to check out at his barge. When he returned the captain had added to the church paraphernalia a portable organ for good measure. He also had ready an unrestricted base leave for his sailor. Mosley tried to thank him, but Graff just waved him off to the truck.

Rumbling along in the truck past mangled greenery and gashes in the earth, First Class Yeoman Mosley carried the embryonic elements of the first Adventist church on Guam. He noticed a warm feeling welling up inside. He finally heard cymbals crashing. Mosley looked down affectionately at his unwieldy load of holy ware. They were, after all, symbols of a world reclaimed, vessels for celebrating that Body which had become invisible for such a long, fearful time.

In time that tent would grow into a fruitful medical, educational, and evangelistic mission. The communion bread would multiply a hundredfold in good soil. But for now Mosley was brim full just holding the seeds on that winding dusty road.

My father, Ramon Mosley, didn't talk that much about his experience during the War; I only managed to coax all the details out of him as I got older. And yet his brave stand was always there for me growing up. This man was willing to put it on the line for his convictions. His belief about the Sabbath did not become the center of his life, he held firmly to the gospel, all the more so as he grew older. But it had been a stand he felt compelled to take. Even in the midst of a world at war, God's will took precedence.

The value of my father's allegiance really sank in the day I saw the James Dean film "Rebel Without a Cause" while in college. There's a scene where Dean is facing a terrible dilemma and seeks help from his father. But the thoroughly conventional man has no useful advice to give. The Dean character, a youth caught in a no man's land between cruel peers and indifferent adults, breaks down and begs his father to say something, anything. He pleads for some kind of guidance. At that point, the awful emptiness of a person who finally sees that his father stands for absolutely nothing becomes apparent. There's nothing there. This wrenching confrontation sends Dean out to his tragic last act of alienation.

Seeing that film made me realize how much it means to have a father who made a stand. My father's allegiance became an eloquent statement for me. Looking back, I can see that I grew up with something to cling to, something straight and true. Right and wrong were woven clearly into the world around me; I always had a place to stand. Just because of the kind of man he was, my father made my religion a bigger and more noble thing.

Great painters have their legacies, generation after generation walks through art galleries and tries to touch their genius. Those who give their full and open allegiance to the Word create a legacy too; generations to come find shelter in their courage.

Chapter Seventeen

ABUSIVE BIGOTS AND ELOQUENT MARTYRS

Now that we've looked at the biblical epic created by those courageously standing for truth, and at the verses of Scripture that give open allegiance a definite shape, it's time to move on in the story. We come to the fascinating tale of believers down through history who have declared their allegiance in various ways. How has the Christian church expressed the authority of the Word? This tradition offers us much that is heroic and much that is petty. But again, it's something we need to learn from if we are to help bring this part of God's truth to a climax. Seeing how open allegiance has been expressed in the past will help us see how to give it a more resounding voice in the future.

In the year A.D. 250, when Decius was Emperor of Rome, a Christian elder named Pionius was led through a large double gate into Smyrna's city square. He was paraded between two colonnades extending for over one hundred yards packed with a holiday crowd, and then taken to a temple to pay sacrifice and eat pagan meats.[1]

Polemon, a temple official, arrived on the scene and explained, "You know, of course, about the Emperor's edict and how it bids you sacrifice to the gods."

"We know the edicts of God, Pionius answered, "in which he bids us worship him alone."

The pagans attempted to pressure Pionius into submitting to their temple rites, but instead of being intimidated he made a speech before the crowd explaining his position. He quoted from certain Greek heroes who had died for philosophy. He protested the unjust treatment of Christians, and warned of a judgment to come.

Later, when officials continued trying to coax him into compromising, Pionius told them, "I wish I could persuade you to be Christians."

They roared with laughter: "You can't make us willing to burn alive!"

Pionius replied, "It is far worse to be burned when you are dead."

While he was escorted back to prison, some in the crowd who'd been impressed by his erudite speech exclaimed, "Ah, what education."

"Not that sort of education," Pionius answered back, wanting them to be impressed by something else. Referring to some recent disasters in the area, said: "Recognize, rather, the education of those famines, deaths and other blows by which you have been tried." He hoped they might look up to the God of heaven out of their sorrows.

His listeners didn't quite get the point. "But you, too, went hungry with us," someone said.

Pionius replied, "But I had hope in God."

He died in that hope, crucified facing East in the city of Smyrna.

Crowds in Pergamum were eager to light the fires and consume another unyielding Christian before a darkening sky rained on them. Their victim, a man named Papylus, though hurried toward the pyre, still gazed fiercely at the truth. "Here the fire burns briefly," he told them, "but there it burns for ever, and by it, God will judge the world. It will drown the sea, the mountains, and the woods. By it, God will judge each human soul."

When a believer named Colluthus was about to be executed, a hopeful judge misjudged the light in his eyes and said, "I can see it in your face; it tells me that you want to be saved. Don't you see the beauty of this pleasant weather? No pleasure will come your way if you kill yourself. But listen to me and you will be saved."

Colluthus answered, "The death which is coming to me is more pleasant than the life which you give."

The Noble and the Scandalous

Pionius, Papylus, and Colluthus were a few of the countless early Christians who took a stand by bearing persuasive witness to a truth bigger than themselves, even as they faced the flames. There was great nobility in the way many followers of Christ declared their allegiance. But among others there was much that was scandalous. Some expressed their allegiance primarily by blasting away at theological opponents.

Alexander, Bishop of Alexandria, couldn't just explain why the views of Arians were unbiblical. He had to launch into loud abuse: "These knaves . . . are driven insane by the devil who works in them."

Bishop Theodoret couldn't quite see eye-to-eye on some issues with Cyril. So when Cyril died the bishop wrote: "The living are delighted. . . . May the guild of undertakers lay a huge, heavy stone on his grave, lest he should come back again and show his faithless mind again. Let him take his new doctrines to Hell, and preach to the damned all day and night."

Jerome wrote this to a man whose doctrine he deemed not completely pure: "You distill from the dunghill of your breast at once the scent of roses and the stench of rotting corpses."

Church historian Paul Johnson comments: "The mind boggles at the lists of offenses with which distinguished ecclesiastics accused each other." They seemed to have had the idea that anyone who held imperfect views of the truth must also be engaged in the worst kind of immorality. So they assumed that their wildest allegations were correct in principle.

From earliest times we have two contrasting ways of declaring allegiance: the eloquence of martyrs who give their lives for the truth, and the virulent abuse of those who attacked others on its behalf. Fortunately, there were also some who made effective stands simply by living a certain way.

An Italian patrician born near Spoleto around the year 480 decided one day to do something about the decadence and depravity of religion at Rome. Benedict left the Eternal City where he was being educated and looked for a quiet place in wild country to the south where he could live simply and meditate on God. Emperor Nero had built a cliff-side palace in that area which was now overgrown. Benedict set up his silent protest there at the scene of so much self-indulgence in the past. He wore a hair shirt and ate only bread that a friend lowered to him in a basket from above the cliff.

Benedict took a stand as an ascetic, but his statement did not center on self-torment. When he heard that an admirer had chained himself in a cave, he sent this message: "The true servant of God is chained not to rocks by iron, but to righteousness by Christ."

Benedict wanted to be useful as well pure. He founded a monastery on the heights of Monte Cassino where monks could become efficient farmers. In time Benedict's reform spread and proved incredibly fruitful. It was his monasteries more than anything else that transformed a Europe in disarray after the fall of Rome into a stable and productive society with a sound agricultural economy. He also managed to awaken an indulgent church to the values of devotion and simplicity—without raising his voice in anger.

Unfortunately, many other angry voices persisted in fighting for their piece of truth. When the church grew as powerful as the state, abusive arguments turned into physical torture. Christians declared their allegiance to the truth by submitting those in error to the horrors of the Inquisition. A very different kind of authority had replaced the winsome voice of the Word.

Battling for the truth also took on a geographic dimension. Crusades to recover the Holy Land from unclean hands aroused Christian passions and mobilized fervent masses. Truth became attached to certain locations, certain sacred sites. And those had to be possessed. The zealous knight had to raise his banner over them, or die trying.

Down through the centuries, a church made powerful has always found it difficult to resist the authority of the sword. But still there were always those who proclaimed a more open allegiance. The Waldensians traveled around Europe preaching New Testament truths in the vernacular and exposing the corruption of many clergy by their simple lifestyle. They rejected most traditions that could not be based on God's Word, so the church persecuted them. Many were slaughtered.

In the fourteenth century, Oxford scholar John Wycliffe based his call for reform on the primitive church described in the New Testament. The church had grown wealthy and overbearing in his day and he made a plea for innocence, purity, and simplicity. Wycliffe protested against the state religion in England which had become a lethargic bureaucracy dedicated to keeping itself fed. He declared that there could be no religious power without virtue. Tithes should be withheld from priests who neglected their duties.

In this, he was taking a stand against his own self-interest as a clergyman. But he saw all around him friars growing fat and monasteries rich in parishes where a wheat cake the size of a man's fist fed wife and children for a day. So he insisted in one typical sermon: "A cup of cold water given with kindness and warm love is a greater gift than all the lands and kingdoms of the church." And in another declared: "If there is a rule most necessary to virtue, it is one that demands the church forsake worldly riches for the riches of God and Christ as the apostles did."[2]

Wycliffe believed the statements of the Bible created one universally applicable truth. The words of Scripture weren't dead on the page; they were still being spoken by God. And so that voice should sound out in living English as well as formal Latin. This conviction led him to begin his famous translation of the Bible that would enlighten all of England.

Bright Words and Needless Bloodshed

One of the most luminous stands in history was made by a Czeck reformer named Jan Hus. He believed that Scripture must be the sole basis for Christian belief. The official church couldn't persuade him to abandon this position, so he was condemned as a heretic. Brought before the bullying of the Council of Constance in 1415, Hus would not recant—"Fearing to offend God and to fall into perjury."

What is most moving about Hus's courageous allegiance is its utter lack of self-righteousness. In his final declaration to the Council, he told them he could not denounce his biblical teachings, but "I would most gladly recant before all the world every falsehood and every error I ever have thought of saying or have said."

At the execution grounds, Hus underwent an elaborate "ceremony of degradation." Officials disrobed him, cut off his hair, and gravely pronounced curses. Hus remarked that he was quite glad to suffer shame for the name of the Lord. When the bishops present intoned a final curse: "We commit your soul to the devil!" Hus replied, "And I commit it to the most merciful Lord Jesus Christ." As the wood and straw piled up to his neck were lit, Hus began singing, "Christ, Thou Son of the living God, have mercy on us." His lips were still moving silently when he died.

Hus stood heroically firm. But he had always been a man always willing to learn. He was, in fact, eager to be shown his mistakes until the end. Hus wrote:

> From the earliest time of my studies I have set up for myself the rule that whenever I discern a sounder opinion in any matter whatsoever, I gladly and humbly abandon the earlier one. For I know that those things I have learned are but the least in comparison with what I do not know.[3]

What a remarkable statement from a man who willfully faced a horrible death rather than endorse "error." It was only because church teachings blatantly contradicted the Word of God that he took an irrevocable stand.

During the age of Reformation, many godly men like Martin Luther made courageous stands on the Word alone. But it became very difficult not to make an armed camp out of your doctrinal position. Allegiance to gospel truth all too often got tangled up with political allegiances. Blood flowed freely on both sides of the Reformation. In the clamor of vengeful voices few heard more tolerant ones.

Giordano Bruno sought to encourage a middle way of reform between the Protestants and Catholics. But in Venice he ran into the Inquisition. He was charged with having stated: "The procedure which the church uses today is not that which the Apostles used, for they converted the people with preaching and the example of good life." For asserting that people should not be tortured into the faith and that the Catholic religion which he loved had need of great reform, he was burned alive as a heretic in Rome.

The Anabaptists also sought a more open allegiance to the Word. Their problem was they insisted on reforming ahead of their time—and so met both Catholic and Protestant opposition. These peculiar believers would not accept the legitimacy of any kind of state-sponsored religion. They wanted to go beyond doctrinal correctness and have a daily walk with Christ, which meant resolutely obeying the "bright and clear words of the Son of God, whose word is truth and whose commandment is eternal life." The Anabaptists, as a rule, would not fight for their beliefs with the sword, or defend themselves when persecuted. In their communities they expressed love concretely, redistributing their wealth to those most needy. Many died eloquently for their New Testament truth.

Some Reformers stood resolutely on the Word, others tried to use the sword to enforce its authority. Even Luther could be vicious; his diatribes against Jews and certain radical Protestant sects are painful to read.

Sometimes the church, wandering from the important principles emphasized in the Word, made tragic, pathetic stands. Reform was a real possibility in the Russian church early in the reign of Czar Alexis. A group of "Zealots of Faith" traveled through the land calling clergy and lay people to sincere spiritual devotion. But the movement broke up over disputes about correct forms of worship. The official church insisted that the sign of the cross be made with three fingers raised, instead of two, and that the three-fold Alleluia, not the two-fold, be sung in worship. Thousands of "Old Ritualists," who believed such liturgical changes signaled an end of the world, sacrificed their lives in opposition.

Other zealous believers have made a stand on the wording of the eucharist and its precise chemistry. Where Scripture only hints, they want to dogmatically declare. And so the clear teaching of the Bible about salvation in Christ is overshadowed by more polemics, more angry debate, more needless bloodshed.

The Word Made Flesh Again

In the nineteenth century, men like George Whitefield and John Wesley declared their allegiance to the living Word against a lifeless orthodoxy that stifled the spirit. The Word needed to be made flesh again; it had hardened into dogma in the established churches where clergymen gave dry dissertations to parishioners nodding off to sleep in agreement.

The Church wanted exposition of the Word carefully regulated.

John Wesley believed its authoritative call should be spread everywhere. He declared his allegiance: "God in Scripture commands me according to my power to instruct the ignorant, reform the wicked, confirm the virtuous. Man forbids me to do this in another's parish; that is, in effect, to do it at all, seeing I have now no parish of my own, nor probably ever shall. Whom then shall I hear: God or man?"

Wesley took a definite stand, all over England, traveling over 250,000 miles in his evangelistic career and preaching some forty thousand sermons. He converted thousands of the spiritually starving and faced violent opposition. The gentry, who feared any kind of revival among the "lower orders of people" incited mobs against him.

Wesley was often beaten by these crowds, but even in the midst of riots he maintained his stand. Some of the most violent troublemakers were won over by his self-possession and earnestness. Once when a mob had beaten him until blood was flowing from open wounds, he managed to gain their attention and began a sermon. Unfortunately he soon lost his voice and the crowd set on him again. However, he began praying at the top of his lungs, and one ruffian listening to the holy words emerging from that bloodied mouth, stepped forward and said, "Sir, I will spend my life for you. Follow me, and not one soul here shall touch a hair of your head."

Wesley was a courageous man with enough drive and stamina to foment a religious revolution in England. But he relied on only one kind of authority: the power of the gospel to transform. Wesley always attempted to persuade; he reasoned from Scripture, always looking a mob in the face, never meeting violence with any force other than the Word. When an angry crowd tried to break up his meeting at St. Ives, he went out to confront them: "I went into the midst and brought the head of the mob to the desk. I received but one blow on the side of the head, after which we reasoned the case, till he grew milder and milder and at length undertook to quiet his companions."[4]

Against the Tide

In 1939, a young German theologian on a lecture tour in America was urged by his friends to take up some safe work in the States and not return to the deteriorating situation in his homeland. But he couldn't. His diary explains simply: "The short prayer in which we thought of our German brothers almost overwhelmed me." He decided to take a stand with fellow believers about to be engulfed in the madness of Nazism and departed on one of the last ships to leave for Germany before the war.

Dietrich Bonhoeffer became a leader of the "Confessing Church" which resisted the philosophy of the brown-shirted fanatics of a new era. Because of his participation in a plot against Hitler, Bonhoeffer was captured, imprisoned, and executed shortly before World War II ended. In his "Letters and Papers from Prison" one gets a glimpse of the source of this man's courageous stand against a tide that overwhelmed most of his Christian contemporaries.

Many of his letters reflect on the meaning of Bible passages he'd been studying. He talked of "a way of seeing the God of the Bible, who wins power and space in the world by his weakness." Scripture was more than just a source of theology for Bonhoeffer; it remained his very personal companion and comfort:

> The heavy air raids, especially the last one, when the windows of the sick-bay were blown out by the land mine, and bottles and medicine supplies fell down from the cupboards and shelves, and I lay on the floor in the darkness with little hope of coming through the attack safely, led me back quite simply to prayer and the Bible.[5]

Bonhoeffer wrote this to a young man home on leave with his wife: "I am very glad you will be able to read the Bible together again morning and evening; it will be a great help to you, not only for these present days, but for the future." He followed his own advise: "I am reading the Bible straight through from cover to cover, and have just got as far as Job, which I am particularly fond of. I read the Psalms every day, as I have done for years; I know them and love them more than any other book."

Bonhoeffer reacted to life through the Word. One of his predecessors in the cell had scribbled over the floor an ironic note: "In 100 years it will all be over." Reflecting on the feeling that time spent in that prison was a tragic blank, he wrote: "'My times are in thy hand' (Psalm 31:15) is the Bible's answer. But in the Bible there is also the question that threatens to dominate everything here: 'How long, O Lord?' (Psalm 13)" Bonhoeffer would conclude: "If this earth was good enough for the man Jesus Christ, if such a man as Jesus lived, then, and only then, has life a meaning for us."

An English officer imprisoned with Bonhoeffer during his last weeks remembered him this way: "Bonhoeffer . . . was all humility and sweetness; he always seemed to me to diffuse an atmosphere of happiness, of joy in every smallest event in life, and of deep gratitude for the mere fact that he was alive. . . . He was one of the very few men that I have ever met to whom God was real and close."

Here and Now

Clarence Jordan, a Baptist pastor in the American South, decided to take a stand on a Greek word: *koinonia,* fellowship. He believed that the fellowship early Christians practiced—pooling their possessions, sharing their lives and their spiritual commitment, bearing each others burdens, and helping the poor—was worthy of imitation in the twentieth century.

Jordan also took seriously the biblical passages that demanded brotherhood, peacemaking, reconciliation, and love for one's enemies. The Sermon on the Mount was, for him, not a lovely speech to be honored in the abstract, but a command of Christ that must be put into practice here and now. Here was Sumter County, Georgia. Now was November of 1942.

Jordan gathered a few like-minded believers around him and began to build Koinonia Farm on 440 treeless, eroded acres near Americus. They plowed and fertilized the land until it yielded good crops, raised corn and hogs, set up an egg marketing cooperative and helped a number of neighboring farmers start their own poultry flocks. They planted apple, pecan, peach, walnut, pear, plum, fig and apricot trees and dug a large vegetable garden; there was always an abundance to share with neighbors—White and Black. They raised a dairy herd and established a "cow library" from which poor families could check out a cow, milk her, and return her for another. They conducted vacation Bible school and Sunday School for the kids near them, mostly Black. They welcomed anyone into their farm who was willing to try Koinonia.

How did the good citizens of Sumter County respond?

They organized a boycott to prevent the farm from selling its produce and buying necessary supplies. They lobbed explosives into their roadside market, and harassed children from Koinonia in the public schools. They destroyed the farm's beehives and cut down three hundred apple, peach, and pecan trees. They set fire to farm buildings and rode by in their cars night after night firing shotguns toward the houses.

Then the leading citizens of Americus paid Pastor Jordan and his colleagues an official visit. They politely asked them to leave the area to avoid inciting any further violence.

The idea that the fellowship Christ commanded might include people of color proved an unbearable outrage to most of Sumter County's white residents. For them, the convention that the races should sleep, eat, learn, and worship separately loomed as large as a statute carved on Sinai. The explicit appeals of Christ to transcend racial barriers trickled away unnoticed.

Southern Georgia, among many other places at the time, suffered from what we might call nominal fundamentalism. It took the worst from two worlds, the secular and religious. It cherished the most flagrant of anti-Christian hatreds toward those on the outside. Yet it sought unquestioned authority for this in selected fragments of Scripture torn from their context.

Clarence Jordan could not ignore the weight of evidence from the Bible. To deny his calling would have required him to "tear out of the New Testament all those pages that proclaim the universality of the Christian brotherhood." The whole weight of Christ's teaching had moved him to those 440 acres near Americus. The Master's words were the source, not just the justification, of his vision. And so his stand made a difference in the end. It lives as "Cotton Patch Evidence" of the authority and vitality of the Word. It is artful goodness that still speaks.[6]

And so we have these many and varied witnesses to the authority of the Word. It's a great tradition of people willing to lay down their lives for it, and a frightening history of people willing to kill others over it.

Intolerance has been a big problem for those adhering to absolute religious truth. Today most of our contemporaries pride themselves on tolerance. But often it's a rather cheap variety: the tolerance of people who don't believe much of anything. People don't war over theology only because they don't take it very seriously. But they find plenty of other "important" things to fight about.

The tolerance that matters is found in people who do take religious truth seriously, who do believe that an authoritative Word has eternal consequences, and yet who refuse to force others under it. They bear witness to its power to win, and no other power.

Looking back on our tradition of eloquent martyrs and abusive bigots, we must ask how we can express the authority of the Word in our world. The Adventist Church has a strong tradition of holding up God's truth, the whole truth. To make that truth ring out we need to demonstrate an open allegiance to it. We need to show that we can take a strong stand and also remain teachable. We need to show that we can defend the truth and also learn from others. We need to show that we can expend our greatest energies on what is most essential in God's Word.

In order for God's truth to prevail in the end, it must do so through our open allegiance. In order for truth to come to a climax, it must progress through our open hearts and minds.

That's how we can make the truth winsome. That's how we can bring a wonderful tradition of artful goodness to a climax.

Standing in the Gap

The American and European "enemy nationals" ordered to an internment camp in Shantung Province by Japanese occupation forces in 1943 were a widely varied lot who had to endure months of boredom, frustration, overcrowding, and fear. Personalities clashed; tempers flared. The two groups thrown into the sharpest relief were the businessmen and the missionaries. They held each other in strictest contempt. Petty squabbles multiplied. The businessmen couldn't understand why the missionaries had to sing hymns at six in the morning. The missionaries were bothered by the others chattering late at night about their "lurid escapades."

Only one individual seemed able to span the gap between these two groups: Eric Liddel, a missionary from Scotland. He was described by an internee as "without a doubt the person most in demand and most respected and loved in camp," A Russian prostitute in camp would later recall that Liddell was the only man who'd ever done anything for her without wanting to be repaid in kind. When she first came into camp, alone and snubbed, he put up some shelves for her.

Another internee recalled, "He had a gentle, humorous way of soothing ruffled tempers and bringing to one's mind some bygone happiness or the prospect of some future interest round the corner 'when we got out.' "

At one irate meeting of the internees everybody was demanding that someone else do something about the restless youngsters in camp who were getting into trouble. Liddell came up with a solution. He organized sports, crafts, and classes for the kids, and began spending his evenings with them.

But he would not oversee games on Sunday. Liddell had grown up believing he should keep that day holy to the Lord. In fact this former world-class sprinter, portrayed in the film *Chariots of Fire*, had sacrificed a gold medal at the 1924 Olympics in his favored event, the 100 meters, because the race was scheduled on Sunday. Though pressured by everyone from his coach to the prince of England, he stood firm. He would not violate principle for Olympic glory. So the team reluctantly scheduled him for the 400 meters, considered a distance race at the time. Liddell, not knowing any better, sprinted all the way around the track and won the gold.

At the Shantung compound, he told the youngsters he was sorry but he couldn't take part in sports on Sunday. Most of them protested and decided to organize their own field hockey game anyway. It ended in a brawl since there was no one to officiate.

The following Sunday Liddel showed up on the field to act as referee—a small act that sheds a great light on his stand. He would not go for Olympic gold if he had to break his Sabbath doing it, but he would keep a handful of imprisoned youngsters from fighting.

Eric Liddel's stand is winsome and eloquent. He didn't use his position as a club, but as an expression of unchanging principles, principles he was nurtured on every morning at 6 A.M. when he tiptoed quietly past sleeping companions, settled down at a low table, and lit a small lamp to illuminate his Bible and notebook.[7]

Chapter Eighteen

QUALITIES AS LUMINOUS AS ART

These then are three primary virtues, the three primary colors, if you please, of the good life. We've traced each one through the Bible, through New Testament teaching, and through the history of the Church. They are strong, deep colors. I believe we can paint great canvases with them. Our religion can greatly expand with light humility, hard honor, and open allegiance.

Each one of these virtues really grows out of the same source. Each one comes from admiring God in some way. Light humility is a direct result of admiring Someone bigger than ourselves. Hard honor happens when we are moved by Christ's great act of honor at Golgotha, when we truly appreciate how widely and deeply He extended grace from the cross. Open allegiance happens when we are awed by God's Word, when we bow before the breadth of God's revealed wisdom.

The root of great virtues is in admiring a great God. Practically speaking, that means that they arise out of the devotional life—spending time in prayer and in the Bible, soaking up the inspiration.

Artists need to look carefully in order to be inspired, in order to create. They need to see something new in a familiar scene. We need to see new things in the Word in order to create artful goodness. But, of

174

course, that's what the Holy Spirit is for, to open the eyes of our hearts.

We need more than just running for a quick promise in an emergency. And we need to treat the Bible as more than a doctrinal textbook. We need, above all, to simply admire, to see something new to appreciate about God.

And Christ is the epicenter of that inspiration. He is the Word perfected, at full strength, flawless and fully expressed. With Jesus we see artful goodness in brilliant color. The canvases on display in four gospel galleries are capable of dazzling us if we look at them closely. They reveal the skill of the greatest Artist of the Spirit. Jesus created something that went far beyond the conventional religion of his contemporaries.

Colors in Balance

Jesus gives us whole revelations, full-color portrayals of divine truth. For us to express a similar wholeness, we need to have those three primary colors in balance. We need each one. Light humility, hard honor, and open allegiance work together to create a many-hued whole.

Start with the deep blue of light humility. That's the color of those who are secure in God's gracious regard. It makes a good background color for hard honor. We need that kind of security in order to honor, in order to extend grace. Goodness twists into all kinds of awkward shapes, trying to be nice, without it.

And hard honor, as richly colored as the dark blood running down Christ's broken flesh on the cross, that quality mixes well with open allegiance. We need to make sure that in all our stands against evil we are also honoring other human beings. Without honor, people often trample on the individuals around them—humanity in particular—while trying to lift up humanity in general.

Open allegiance, in turn, has a striking hue of its own. It's a color that light humility and hard honor need to draw on. Responding to the authority of the Word keeps us moving forward. Open allegiance splashes the bright yellow light of the Word on all our thoughts and deeds. It enables us to take stands, to resist the tide, when necessary. It prevents humility and honor from getting soft and passive.

Each of these three primary qualities is essential in the composition. They are what expand our religious life. Light humility, hard honor, open allegiance. These three primary colors combine and fill us out in full-color. We become balanced human beings growing into the image of

God. These are the colors that can make our Adventism much bigger and much grander—for ourselves and for our contemporaries. I believe they are key elements in the big picture that God wants to put together at the climax of history.

We can make a statement in our world every bit as eloquent as the paintings of the greatest artists. There are some things worth expressing in this world, some things that echo eternally. There are eloquent virtues worth their weight in Rembrandt's colors or the lines of Ingres.

Goodness doesn't have to be conventional or colorless; it doesn't have to be confined to the sidelines trying to avoid evil. It doesn't have to be small. It can become a glorious pursuit.

Whatever you do, Scripture tells us, do it all to the glory of God. Make your acts speak of Him; flesh out His qualities. We can do more than just imitate from a distance; we can become participants in the divine nature. That's an art worth our lifetimes.

As we look intently, with unveiled faces, in the devotional life, we can be "transformed into His likeness with ever-increasing glory." We can be compelled by Christ, laid hold of by our spiritual muse, people who "press toward the goal of the prize of the upward call of God."

This is what we can become as a people nearing the climax of history. We can become artists of the spirit, inspired enough to aim high, hoping to experience "the whole measure of the fullness of Christ." And why not dream? Why not excel? Our God "can do more than we ask or think through the power at work within us." Plugged into the source of creation, we echo His skill and revelation, producing acts of art that God Himself can treasure. Paul wants us to realize "what are the riches of the glory of His inheritance in the saints." God glories in our eloquent virtues. Creativity comes full circle, from master to pupil and back again.

Artful goodness is our calling as children of God. There's no higher one, no other pursuit more valuable. It's this kind of art that really makes the greatest impact, the greatest difference in the world. Just look at a few shining examples.

The Light Humility of Camille Monet[1]

At the age of eighteen, Camille was swept off her feet by a visionary painter named Claude Monet. He was a struggling, impoverished artist at the time and he remained exactly that during the fifteen years they were together. The road to success in nineteenth-century Paris lay through the all-powerful Academy of Fine Arts where painting was taught in the approved style: correct, finished, lifeless. Talented students might someday exhibit their works in the Academy Salon and thus begin to sell.

Claude Monet couldn't bring himself to take that road. He longed to capture the liveliness of things—the interaction of light, color, and shape in one momentary impression.

Camille set up house in a tiny Paris flat and made do with the little money Claude could beg from artist friends. They were often cold and hungry, but she never complained. It was her cheery faith in the worth of his canvases that helped Claude keep going. Yes, someday the world would see, someday recognition would come.

Camille became pregnant. Monet wrote desperate letters, begging, shaming, arguing, demanding help from friends. A few francs trickled in; not enough. He walked the streets with canvases under his arm trying to get a pittance from art dealers for his work. No one was interested.

Camille grew more and more pale. But Monet couldn't give up on his dream. He had to keep painting. She was ill when she gave birth to a sturdy boy they named Jean. The three existed in a bare room without a fire. When the cupboard became empty or Monet's paint supply failed, he would traipse the streets again trying to sell his work. As usual it was Camille's courage and gaiety in the face of hard times that made their desperate straits bearable.

There were a few lulls in the struggle. In the spring of 1868, Monet received 800 francs for a painting. That kept them fed for a while. But the Salon was still rejecting his work. The money ran low; they moved to Normandy where life was cheaper.

Eventually Monet become a leader in the new art movement called Impressionism, but he still couldn't sell his work. There were more hardships, more desperate letters to friends, more disappointments, and always more canvases to paint. "I am the prisoner of my eye," Monet said.

The strain of barely surviving began taking its toll on Camille. She steadily weakened. But in her frailty she somehow could always draw on an inexhaustible well of devotion. Monet was drawn to her more than ever before; but he still could not stop painting. He felt guilty for not taking better care of her, but his obsession drove him on. Surely someone would recognize his work soon. The one thing he did not do was find some way to earn a living in order to adequately care for his wife and son. A job in a shop or office or at the docks might delay his emergence as a great painter. That he could not bear. He could have devoted some time to caricatures or some other kind of popular painting that would earn money, but he didn't see that as an option. Monet believed passionately in his art; he would not compromise it. He had to make the world see his vision.

What he did not see so clearly was the woman who was such a vital part of his art: Camille. He painted her in the fields tall and stately, in their gardens, on the beach, posed with their son Jean. She appeared often on his canvases, but one wonders whether he ever really took the measure of this human being who showed such determined grace and good humor under the most withering of circumstances.

A profound kind of art lay hidden in Camille's sweet selflessness. But it was an art that no one made any sacrifices to preserve. Monet saw only the narrow spectrum of his own particular art. As one biographer put it: "He had, like so many artists, the sense that the less creative can best justify their existence by assisting the original artist." But who was really "less creative"? Camille was very happy to play the role of the person giving her life for the "original artist." But, although she was too self-effacing to realize it, Camille had become an artist of the spirit in her own right.

She carried her humility so lightly. In 1876, Monet painted her as "La Japonaise," dressed in a huge, brilliantly colored kimono. She lifts a fan up beside her face, tilts her head back and looks at us as if caught in a dance. Her bright eyes and querying smile flirt with the viewer. This is still the same cheery girl who fell for a dashing young painter. There are no traces of the woman who had been worn down by years of privation.

If Camille had been some stern-faced matron sacrificing herself because duty to one's husband demanded it, her suffering could be more easily passed over. But this woman loved life. It's the gaiety of her selflessness that makes it so compelling, her ability to appreciate and believe against the odds in the art of another when no one could appreciate her own.

In 1879, though pale and weak, with dark patches spreading in the hollows of her eyes, Camille gave birth to a fine healthy boy, Michel. But she never recovered her strength. The next year, she died of tuberculosis. Camille was 32.

Monet begged enough money to bury her in the little walled cemetery that crowns a hill at Vetheuil. No one is really sure where she lies.

178

Her stone was never inscribed.

A few years later, the breakthrough finally arrived. The public had begun warming to Impressionism and Monet's paintings started selling. His reputation grew.

But Monet struggled for some time with new work. He wrote, "I have scraped off all my latest canvases. I suffer anguish." And later in another location, he said, "I've destroyed six (canvases) since coming here. I've done only one that pleases me. I'm tired of it all."

Monet had only to paint what he pleased and it would sell for almost any price he demanded. But he found himself increasingly restless and bitter. "I work hard," he wrote, "and make myself ill with wretchedness: I'm horribly worried by everything I do."

He probably did not realize what an irreplaceable part of his inspiration Camille had been. One biographer concluded: "With Camille's death, his wonderful eye lost its most powerful creative force. . . . All the warmth, the humanity, the feeling in his pictures came from her."

Monet, as a matter of fact, would go on to paint some of his most famous works, his series of haystacks and water lilies, for example. But a case can be made that he was now indeed merely a prisoner of his eye, and that now it remained a disembodied organ.

The deep blue of Camille's light humility had faded from the canvas. It was she who had created the greatest paintings of all.

The Hard Honor of Johanna Van Gogh[2]

Dr. Felix Rey wrote Theo Van Gogh from his mental hospital at Saint-Remy in the south of France to tell him about his brother. Vincent's condition had worsened. He had attempted to bathe in a coal scuttle, threatened a nurse, and occupied another patient's bed, refusing to get up.

Theo decided he'd better make the trip to the hospital. He'd always tried to sustain Vincent, emotionally and financially. But in the face of this final illness at the hospital, he felt helpless. Theo wrote: "He had, while I was with him, moments in which he acted normally, but then after a short while he slipped off into wanderings on philosophy and theology. It was deeply saddening to witness all this, for from time to time he became conscious of his illness and in those moments he tried to cry—yet no tears came. Poor fighter and poor, poor sufferer."

Vincent was struggling against his manic attacks, knowing they might destroy forever his ability to paint. But he had grown increasingly isolated. The townspeople of Arles where he'd been painting regarded him with hostile suspicion. He'd been a dismal failure with women and now sought comfort only among prostitutes. His physician at the mental hospital offered little hope. The Catholic sisters seemed cool. And always his disease threatened.

In the midst of this enveloping dark, one bright beam of honor shone through—from a most unlikely source. Back in Paris, Theo had married a Dutch woman named Johanna. This woman now had to deal with a brother-in-law whom she knew would drain their meager finances indefinitely. Vincent had been making financial and emotional demands on his brother for years. There were no signs his position would ever improve and plenty of signs that he he'd become a dangerous lunatic. Just a few weeks before he'd tried to stab the artist Gaugin who was staying with him, and then, tormented over his act, he'd cut off his earlobe and given it to a prostitute.

Johanna's response to all this seems to me quite remarkable. She wrote him: "I am now going to tell you a great piece of news, on which we have concentrated a good deal of our attention lately—it is that next winter . . . we hope to have a baby, a pretty little boy—whom we are going to call Vincent, if you will kindly consent to be his godfather. Of course I know we must not count on it too much, and that it may well be a little girl, but Theo and I cannot help imagining that the baby will be a boy."

Johanna had good reason to wish Vincent a quick disappearance. This "artist" had sold exactly two paintings in his lifetime and offered no evidence of being remembered by posterity except for his eccentricities. But Johanna and Theo honored anyway, linking the identity of their first-born child with Vincent's. In those paintings that covered the walls of their home (no one else would have them) they saw a value, something redeemable, something to honor. In "The Potato Eaters" hanging in their sitting room, Vincent had honored the poor like no one before him. These were the people Theo had ministered to so compassionately during his stint as an evangelist.

And so, hemmed in by his private terrors in the asylum, Vincent received this gift from a woman he hardly knew. He wrote back to them both: "Jo's (Johanna's) letter told me a very great piece of news this morning, I congratulate you on it and I am very glad to hear it." He suggested it might be more appropriate to name the baby after its grandfather considering "the circumstances."

After the birth of the child, a boy which the parents christened Vincent, his uncle expressed his joy by painting what he wrote was "big branches of almond-trees in blossom against a blue sky." A few weeks later he took an overnight train to Paris and there Johanna saw him for the first time: "I had expected a sick man," she recalled, "but here was a sturdy, broad-shouldered man with a healthy color, a smile on his face and a very resolute appearance." For his part, Vincent found his sister-in-law "intelligent, warm-hearted and unaffected."

Johanna describes the moment all three had been waiting for: "Theo drew him into the room where our little boy's cradle was. . . . Silently the two brothers looked at the quietly sleeping baby—both had tears in their eyes. Then Vincent turned smilingly to me and said, pointing to the simple crocheted cover on the cradle, 'Don't cover him with too much lace, little sister.' "

Vincent spent three days with the family, "cheerful and lively," basking in this island of loving calm and in the new life of his namesake. Tragically, after his return to southern France, Vincent was enveloped by the old demons again. Theo and Johanna's act of honor wasn't enough to save him from eventual suicide, but the gift did sink in for a while. In one of his last letters he wrote, "I am so glad to have seen Jo and the little one. . . ."

Hard honor. Johanna naming her child Vincent, projecting health and wholeness toward a tormented, difficult man—this is an act of artful goodness every bit as luminous as the painter's brilliant sunflowers fetching their millions at Christie's.

Reign of Terror[3]

Early in the morning of the second of May, 1808, the citizens of Madrid rose up in revolt against the soldiers of Napoleon who had occupied their land. Men and women took to the streets with whatever weapons they could muster and attacked French troops. The Spaniards fought bravely but were soon overwhelmed by disciplined soldiers who counterattacked with cavalry and artillery pieces.

In the afternoon an uneasy silence hung over the city, broken only by the sound of reprisals. Groups of citizens were rounded up and executed by firing squads. At first only those carrying weapons were to be shot, but soon the killing became more and more indiscriminate. It lasted until early morning of the following day.

This revolt was only the first in a series of disastrous conflicts that broke out on Spanish soil. One man documented that horror with an almost obsessive persistence: Francisco Goya, regarded now as the greatest artistic genius of his age.

One of Goya's most famous paintings, "The Third of May," recalls the execution of the 'Madrilenos'—people of Madrid. A faceless line of soldiers prepares to fire into a terrified group of citizens; the solid row of uniformed executioners bent implacably over their rifles contrasts with the wild gestures of those about to die. One lurches forward to pray, one covers face with hands, one stares in disbelieving shock, and a kneeling, white-shirted man, the center of the composition, spreads his arms wide and stares aghast, his stance screaming a mixture of supplication and protest.

"The Third of May" was Goya's way of taking a stand. He spoke powerfully about tyranny and suffering. His image still moves us today. During that bloody period, Goya created a series of prints called "Los Desastres de la Guerra," (The Disasters of War) which expressed what he had seen and felt. The prints are unique in their graphic depiction of cruelty and in their oddly direct titles. Goya seems to want to shake us by the neck with these scenes.

Soldiers hack up a spread-eagled body; the title reads "What More Can One Do?" "Barbarians!" is his epithet for two soldiers firing on a man tied around a tree. Men, women, and children mowed down by rifle fire is, "One Cannot Look." A couple covering their faces as they look on a mound of corpses is called "Bury and Be Quiet."

But Goya would not be quiet. He shows us war at its most brutal. Unfortunately the terror continued on for Goya and his countrymen in the years after Napoleon fell and the Spanish Bourbons returned to power. They proved they could be as savagely repressive as the French. Goya had ever more disasters to document.

He also had even more despair to deal with. His harshly eloquent stand against the cruelty and inhumanity around him didn't seem to make much difference. He withdrew more and more into his own world and began executing a series of what are called "Black Paintings" on the walls of his small farmhouse near Madrid. They were very private statements, intended to be viewed by himself in solitude.

Goya pictured "Saturn Devouring One of His Sons," in which a wild-eyed, shadowy man claws into a tiny figure and tears off its arm in his mouth. Skeletal animal-humans cavort in "The Food of the Witches." Women sit in a worshipful circle around a large-horned goat-god in "The Witches' Sabbath."

All of this intensely personal work was dominated by scenes that can best be described as nightmares. Goya had made a forceful statement about the inhumanity of war, but he was also tormented by a very private savagery. The same demonic forces he saw out there butchering his fellow citizens lurked in his own mind. He had stood against evil, but when he looked inside he could find no real alternative, no greater image. Its unending reign of terror overwhelmed his spirit.

It would take another man to show us how to make a more meaningful stand amid the horrors of war.

The Open Allegiance of Desmond Doss[4]

On the fifth of May, 1945, the advance of the 77th Division of American troops through Okinawa was still held up by stubborn resistance on the Maeda Escarpment. This promontory running almost the entire breadth of the island rose steeply from the central valley and peaked in a sheer rock cliff, from thirty to fifty feet high. The Japanese had fortified the escarpment with pillboxes and a maze of tunnels and managed to turn back several all-out assaults. Now orders came down from 10th Army headquarters that the ridge was to be taken at all costs. The 1st Battalion, spearheaded by Company B, was assigned to attack a pillbox anchoring the Japanese line. Company B's Captain Frank Vernon tried to prepare his men for what he knew would be the fight of their lives. Some were new recruits sent in to replace the heavy casualties Company B sustained on the island. There was one man Vernon especially wanted along on this mission.

He walked over to a soldier who sat nursing a leg he'd injured in a fall over the cliff and told him about the orders. "Doss," Vernon said, "I know you don't have to go on this mission. But the men would like to have you with them and so would I."

It had not always been like that. Back in boot camp with the 77th, the other recruits ridiculed Desmond Doss as "holy Jesus." When he quietly read the Bible and prayed at his bunk each evening they threw boots or yelled obscenities. Doss just didn't fit in; the skinny kid with glasses was too much of a straight arrow.

When drafted, Doss had registered I-A-O and assumed he'd be assigned to a medical unit. Instead he found himself in an infantry unit and was ordered to take a rifle. Doss could not. On the wall of his family's living room in Lynchburg, Virginia hung a framed scroll illustrating the Ten Commandments which he'd studied in awe ever since the time he could drag a chair over and climb up for a look. The sixth commandment, "Thou shalt not kill," pictured a murderous Cain standing with a dagger over his prostrated, bleeding brother.

Doss wanted to obey God's commands, even with a world at war. He'd been taught, and still believed, that they were eternally valid. But he also wanted to serve his country; he believed in the values of a democracy that was pitted against Nazi tyranny. When a shipyard official where he worked suggested that he could get a deferment as someone "essential to industry" Doss declined. He would accept the call to service. But he would also try to express his greater loyalty to God, so he signed up as a noncombatant.

As a result, Doss had to face a succession of superior officers who demanded that he carry a weapon. They shouted and pleaded; he respectfully refused. Finally a friendly chaplain straightened out the confusion and Doss began training as a medic.

He joined the men of Company B out in the desert of Arizona as they were being whipped into shape on long marches in the withering heat. At first they didn't think much of the soft-spoken "objecter" with his ever-present Bible either. But he soon won their respect for his toughness in the field and skill in caring for their injuries.

Their respect grew during combat on the island of Guam when he insisted on going out on dangerous night patrols with the "dogfaces" instead of sticking to the battalion aid station. He knew even the bravest of soldiers has a horror of being wounded and left behind to the mercy of the enemy.

Their admiration turned to something approaching awe on the Philippine island of Leyte during fierce jungle fighting when Doss scurried about caring for the wounded under fire, seemingly impervious to Japanese bullets. For his continual bravery during the campaign superiors recommended him for the Bronze Star.

It was with good reason that Captain Vernon wanted Desmond Doss along on the mission to take the Maeda Escarpment, though he hated to ask it. Doss didn't hesitate. "I'll go, Captain," he told Vernon. But then he asked permission to finish studying his Sabbath School lesson. The Captain started to object. The entire American advance in Okinawa was hung up at this one spot. But then he looked down at Doss's face and saw eyes sunk deep into dark sockets from exhaustion. The man hadn't even had time to change his cotton uniform now stiff with the dried blood of the men he'd rescued during previous assaults.

Vernon nodded, "We'll wait for you," and walked off.

Doss's sunken eyes had seen a great deal during the previous months: men with chests torn open by shell fragments, men disemboweled, pleading to be shot. He'd crawled among blood-drenched dismembered bodies feeling neck arteries for signs of life; he'd watched helplessly as his best friend bled to death beside him. Doss was surrounded by the disasters of war; all the horrors that Francisco Goya documented so fervently and despairingly pressed against him—and took their toll.

A few days earlier, Doss found himself squatting beside a can of gasoline he'd lit, staring at the flame in a daze, with tears running down his cheeks. GIs usually lit such a fire to warm up their rations, but Doss wasn't hungry. He knew he had to snap out of it, stop thinking about all his dead buddies. He'd grown edgy and irritable. His hands shook. His voice sometimes broke.

At times like this, he tried to focus on his trust in the Lord. He had to keep the madness at bay with the good Word; he could still be loyal to it, no matter what. He still had something to say, even in the midst of a terror that seemed to envelope the whole world: he could preserve life; yes life was worth preserving.

For Doss, that meant all life. Once he tried to treat two dying Japanese soldiers, but a couple of GI's made him back off at rifle point. On Guam, he managed to rescue a few seriously wounded native Chamorros. A buddy asked him, "Haven't you got enough to do, taking care of our own men? Why try to resurrect these natives?"

"Because it's not up to me to judge whether one of God's children should live or die," Doss answered. "I believe that I should do everything in my power to help all men hold on to life."

"Suppose they aren't fit to live?"

Doss explained, "Well, the way I look at it is that anybody who isn't fit to live surely isn't fit to die!"

Try your best to preserve life. This was what he was trying to cling to desperately. He had to keep in touch with the Word, with that better image, which enabled him to make a meaningful stand in the midst of

"Bury and Be Quiet," "Barbarians!" and "What More Can One Do?" And so Doss, quite unaware that he was holding up the war, finished his Bible reading, bowed his head for a few moments of prayer, and then stood up, testing his leg. He was relieved to find that it supported him.

The men of Company B, covered by sweeping fire from the rear, moved up and over the escarpment and managed to throw a few explosives down the pillbox hole. A mighty rumble shook the entire hill; they'd set off an ammunition dump underground. They'd also set off the Japanese counterattack. Okinawa's defenders poured out of holes everywhere, screaming, firing rifles, and tossing grenades. Captain Vernon ordered the men to dig in but they were soon overwhelmed by sheer numbers. Retreat turned into panic as soldiers rushed madly back toward the cliff; many were cut down by enemy fire.

Only one man remained on top doing his job: Desmond Doss, tending to the fallen amid a terrifying concentration of artillery, mortar, and machine-gun fire. Alone on the escarpment, he began pulling casualties from where they'd been cut down to the edge and then scurrying back for more. Then he rigged a litter with rope, slipping the legs of one of the most seriously wounded men through the two loops of a bowline, passing the rope around the man's chest and tying another bowline there. He looped the long end of the rope around a shattered tree stump and slowly lowered his comrade down the cliff to safety. In this way Doss managed to move the wounded, one after the other, from the escarpment. The slope where he worked was partly shielded from enemy fire, but he had to stand up during part of the lowering process and his head and shoulders were often exposed. No one could figure out why the heavy gunfire never struck him.

Doss remained on the escarpment until he'd lowered every wounded man to the soldiers waiting below. He was preserving life with a vengeance; seventy-five men that day would owe their lives to him. Later, for his "outstanding gallantry far above and beyond the call of duty," Desmond Doss was awarded the Congressional Medal of Honor by President Truman.

A few days after his heroic stand on the escarpment, Doss was wounded by a sniper and had to be evacuated by ambulance. As he was driven away, the medic suddenly gasped, "My Bible, I've lost my Bible!"

"It's OK," the driver said, "They'll get you one on the ship."

But Doss wanted *his* Bible, the one that had carried him through the long terror. He made the driver promise he'd pass the word to his friends at the battalion aid station, asking them to look for it. Word did get back to Company B and all the men fanned out over the battefield, pausing in their war to poke around shell holes and under debris, keeping an eye out for booby traps and snipers, retracing Doss's last steps, until they found the small leather-bound book that their comrade, the skinny, bespeckled "preacher" they had come to respect and love, regarded so earnestly as the Word of God.

Desmond Doss stands among those whose acts are eloquent as art. He was not trying to establish a rationally perfect pacifist position. Ethicists could argue at length about the consistency of Doss's stand in the Pacific. Wasn't he just as much a part of the war as those carrying rifles? But this man was making a statement, the finest he could under the circumstances, that life is worth preserving. He was willing to keep that saying that under the most dangerous conditions imaginable. Doss gives us a canvas to look at, one every bit as powerful as Goya's "Third of May."

Yes, some people do make of "simple goodness" a glorious enterprise, men and women whose virtue is anything but small. And it's not just the obvious heroes like Desmond Doss. Johanna van Gogh's act of honor speaks to us as well, and illuminates us as the best words of arty try to do. Spurgeon's sensitive grace with his orphans, Eric Liddell's winsome care for unruly teenagers in an internment camp, Hudson Taylor's faith ventures in innermost China—they all make the word bigger for us; they embody truths that are often hidden.

These people had a passion to express something. They are a great cloud of witnesses around us. They urge us to follow in the race; they ask us to pursue the holy with the ardor of a painter like Albert Ryder who wrote of his craft: "The artist needs but a roof, a crust of bread, and his easel, and all the rest God gives him in abundance. He must live to paint and not paint to live."

We dare not make a lesser commitment. Artful goodness must be the passion of our innermost selves. It will greatly expand our lives. It will make our religion immeasurably bigger. It will take us as a people to the climax of history, when the kingdom of God fills up the heavens with the glory of God.

Each of us can join in the great pursuit of the eloquent virtues today. Each of us has a brush stroke to make on that greatest of canvases.

Sources

Most Scripture quotations in this book are from The Holy Bible: New International Version, copyright 1973, 1978, 1984 by the International Bible Society, and published by Zondervan Bible Publishers. Other versions used include the New American Standard Bible, the Revised Standard Version, the New English Bible, and The New Testament in Modern English, translated by J.B. Phillips.

Chapter One

1. *A Portrait of the Artist as a Young Man,* James Joyce (Penguin Books, 1975).

Chapter Two

1. Quotations from artists: *Artists on Art*, edited by Robert Goldwater and Marco Treves (New York: Random House, 1972).
2. Romans 8:2.
3. 1 Corinthians 12:13, KJV.
4. Ephesians 5:18, 19.
5. Galatians 3:2, RSV.
6. Colossians 3:16.
7. 1 Corinthians 2:10.
8. Ephesians 1:17,18.
9. Romans 8:4.
10. 1 John 1:4, NAS.
11. *In God's Underground*, Richard Wurmbrand (New York, London, Toronto: Bantam Books, 1977).

Chapter Three

1. *2500 Anecdotes for All Occasions,* edited by Edmund Fuller (Garden City, New York: Doubleday & Company, 1961), 70.
2. *The Oxford Book of Literary Anecdotes,* edited by James Sutherland (New York: Pocket Books, 1976), 73.
3. *Desert Calling,* Anne Fremantle (London: Hollis & Carter, 1950).

Chapter Four

1. *Conversions,* edited by Hugh T. Kerr and John M. Mulder (Grand Rapids, Michigan: William B. Eerdmans, 1983).

Chapter Five

1. 1 Samuel 11:13.
2. Psalm 51:17.
3. Psalm 131:1, 2.
4. 2 Chronicles 12:6.
5. 2 Chronicles 26:16.
6. 2 Kings 22:19.
7. 2 Chronicles 36:12.
8. Daniel 4:34, 37.
9. John 3:27-30.

10. Matthew 18:4.

Chapter Six
1. Matthew 18:4.
2. 1 Peter 5:6.
3. Colossians 3:12.
4. John 13:3, 5, NASB.
5. Philippians 3:5-9.
6. 1 Corinthians 1:13.
7. 1 Corinthians 15:10.
8. 2 Corinthians 11:30.
9. Philippians 4:12, 13.
10. 2 Corinthians 6:8-10.
11. *Path to the Heart,* Glenn A. Coon (Hagerstown, Md.: Review and Herald Publishing Association, 1958), 100-104.

Chapter Seven
1. *Pagans and Christians,* Robin Lane Fox (New York: Alfred A. Knopf, Inc. 1987), 337; *A History of Christianity,* Paul Johnson, (New York: Atheneum, 1977).
2. *Bonaventure,* The Classics of Western Spirituality, translation and introduction by Ewert Cousins (New York: Paulist Press, 1978), 132.
3. *Bonaventure,* 232.
4. *Butler's Lives of the Saints,* vol. IV, edited by Herbert Thurston & Donald Attwater (New York: P. J. Kenedy & Sons, 1962), 111-120.
5. *Confessions and Enchriridon,* Agustine, translated and edited by Albert C. Outler (Philadephia: Westminster, 1955), "Confessions," Book Two, 57.
6. *Man Discovers God,* Sherwood Eddy (Freeport N.Y.: Books for Libraries Press, 1968), 100.
7. *An Anthology of Mysticism,* 107.
8. *Showings* (The Classics of Western Spirituality), Julian of Norwich, translated and with an introduction by Edmund Colledge and James Walsh (New York: Paulist Press, 1978), 288.
9. *The Practice of the Presence of God,* Brother Lawrence, (Springdale, Penn.: Whitaker House, 1982).
10. *The Protestant Mystics,* selected and edited by Anne Fremantle (Boston: Little, Brown & Co., 1964), 73.
11. *The Protestant Mystics,* 299.
12. *J. Hudson Taylor,* Dr. and Mrs. Howard Taylor, (Chicago: Moody Press, 1977).
13. *Chosen Vessels: Portraits of Ten Outstanding Christian Men,* Harry Blamires (Vine Books, 1985).

Chapter Eight
1. *Chivalry,* Maurice Keeb (New Haven, Conn.: Yale University Press, 1984).
2. *Southern Honor,* Bertram Wyatt-Brown, (New York: Oxford University Press, , 1982).
3. *Time,* November 4, 1985, 31-32.
4. *Spurgeon,* Arnold Dallimore (Chicago: Moody Press, 1984).

Chapter Nine
1. *The Myths of Greece and Rome,* H. A. Guerber (London: George G. Harrap & Co., 1938).
2. Genesis 15.

Chapter Ten
1. 1 Samuel 14:6.
2. Samuel 24:11.
3. Ruth 2:8, 9.
4. Acts 9:17.

Chapter Eleven
1. Romans 12:10, RSV.
2. 1 Peter 2:17, RSV.
3. 1 Peter 3:7, RSV.
4. See Ephesians 5:22-33.
5. See Ephesian 6:1-9.
6. 1 Peter 3:8, NASB.
7. 1 John 4:10.
8. Galatians 3:28.
9. 2 Corinthians 5:14-17.
10. 2 Corinthians 7:3, NASB.
11. *Reader's Digest,* May 1986, 136-140; *Guideposts,* January 1986.

Chapter 12
1. *A History of Christianity,* Paul Johnson, (New York: Atheneum, 1977), 74, 75.
2. *A History of Christianity,* Paul Johnson, (New York: Atheneum, 1977), 74, 75.
3. *A History of Christianity,* Paul Johnson, (New York: Atheneum, 1977), 74, 75.
4. *The Life and Writings of the Historical Saint Patrick,* R.P.C. Hanson (Seabury Press, , 1983).
5. *Bonaventure,* 195.
6. *Bright Legacy,* edited by Ann Spangler (Ann Arbor, Mich.: Servant Books, , 1983).
7. *By Their Blood,* James Hefley and Marti Hefley (Milford, Mich.: Mott Media, 1979), 570-576.

Chapter 13
1. *Here I Stand,* Roland H. Bainton (New American Library, 1950).

Chapter 14
1. John 13:34.
2. *Ben Israel,* Arthur Katz (Plainfield, N. J.: Logos International, 1970), 86-88.
3. Galatians 1:12.
4. 1 Peter 1:21, NEB.
5. 2 Timothy 3:16.
6. Matthew 7:29.
7. 1 Corinthians 1:17.

Chapter 15
1. 1 Kings 22.
2. Jeremiah 21:8, 9.

Chapter 16
1. 2 Corinthians 13:8, NASB.
2. 1 Thessalonians 3:8.
3. 2 Timothy 2:15.
4. Mark 2:27.

Sources

5. Mark 3.
6. Hebrews 5:14.
7. 2 Corinthians 11:3.
8. 1 Corinthians 8:7.
9. Romans 14:1.
10. Romans 14:3.
11. Romans 14:5.
12. 1 Thessalonians 2:7.
13. Ephesians 6:13.
14. *Chosen Vessels,* Charles Turner (Ann Arbor, Mich.: Servant Publications, 1985).
15. 2 Timothy 3:16.
16. Romans 12:2.
17. *J. Hudson Taylor, God's Man in China,* Dr. and Mrs. Howard Taylor (Moody Press, Chicago, 1977).

Chapter 17
1. These stories and quotes of the early martyrs and church leaders are from
A History of Christianity, Paul Johnson, (New York: Atheneum, 1977).
2. *The Perilous Vision of John Wyclif,* Louis Brewer Hall, (Chicago: Nelson-Hall, 1983).
3. *Jan Hus: A Biography,* Matthew Spinka (Princeton University Press, 1968)
4. *John Wesley,* Basil Miller (Minneapolis, Minn.: Bethany Fellowship, l943).
5. *Letters and Papers from Prison,* Dietrich Bonhoeffer (New York: Macmillan, 1970).
6. *The Cotton Patch Evidence,* Dallas Lee (New York: Harper & Row Publishers, 1971).
7. *The Flying Scotsman,* Sally Magnusson (New York: Quartet Books, 1981).

Chapter 18
1. *Monet,* Charles Merrill Mount (New York: Simon and Schuster, 1966).
Camille, A Study of Claude Monet, C. P. Weekes (London: Sidgwick and Jackson Ltd., 1962).
2. *The World of Van Gogh,* Robert Wallace and the Editors of Time-Life Books (New York: Time-Life Books, 1969).
Van Gogh, Pierre Cabanne (Englewood Cliffs, N. J.: Prentice-Hall, 1963.
Van Gogh: A Self-portrait, letters selected by W. H. Auden (New York: E. P. Dutton, 1963).
3. *Goya,* Fred Licht (New York: Universe Books, 1979).
Goya in Perspective, Fred Licht (Englewood Cliffs, New Jersey: Prince-Hall, 1973).
4. *The Unlikeliest Hero,* Booton Herndon (Nampa, Idaho: Pacific Press®, 1967).

If you enjoyed this book, you'll enjoy these as well:

Burned Out on Being Good
Steven Mosley. A book to help Christians get over "religion burnout" and get on fire for God again. Shows the distinction between being stuck in a religion of avoidance and being in a religion that focuses on a personal relationship with God. Makes Christianity positive and practical.
0-8163-1578-7. Paperback. US$8.99, Can$12.99.

It's Time to Stop Rehearsing What We Believe and Start Looking at What Difference it Makes
Reinder Bruinsma. In this fresh look at Adventist beliefs, the secretary of the Trans-European Division addresses what difference it makes to have doctrines. This book will captivate people who question how doctrine applies to every-day life issues.
0-8163-1401-2. Paperback. US$9.99, Can$14.49.

Searching for a God to Love
Chris Blake. Searching for a God to Love is for our relatives and friends who haven't come to God yet. They're smart. Fun. Skeptical. They're "good people." And they may be lost forever.
This book is about God. Not the one shrouded in rhetoric, condemnation, and pious, proof-text reasoning. It's about the God who is more vast and wondrous than any of us can fathom, written in language seekers can understand.
0-8163-1719-4. Paperback. US$11.99, Cdn$17.99

Order from your ABC by calling **1-800-765-6955**, or get online and shop our virtual store at **www.adventistbookcenter.com**.
- Read a chapter from your favorite book
- Order online
- Sign up for e-mail notices on new products